Han and T'ang Murals

2 Nos. 80 and 89, from Wei-Chin tombs at Chia-yü-kuan, Kansu Province (see pp. 73 and 76)

Han and T'ang Murals discovered in tombs in the People's Republic of China and copied by contemporary Chinese painters

Jan Fontein and Wu Tung

Museum of Fine Arts
Boston

Library of Congress Catalogue
Card No. 76-44478
ISBN 0-87846-102-7

Type set by Dumar Typesetting,
Dayton, Ohio
Color separations by
Techno-colour Co. Inc., Montreal

Printed by
Foremost Lithographers
Providence, R.I.
Designed by Carl F. Zahn

Museum of Fine Arts, Boston
October 5 - November 22, 1976

Chinese Culture Foundation of San Francisco

Cover illustrations: nos. 69, 83, 64, 36, and 60

Contents

6 No. 4, from an Eastern Han tomb at P'ing-lu, Shansi Province (see p. 25)

Preface

FOR the traveling exhibition of archaeological finds from the People's Republic of China that captivated the imagination of the American museum-going public last year, a few copies of wall paintings were chosen to illustrate the cultural and social background of that magnificent array of treasures. The copies in the present, much more modest enterprise constitute the core of what is primarily an educational exhibition, including, as well, some photographic reproductions of wall paintings. It has been organized by the Museum of Fine Arts in cooperation with the Liaison Office of the People's Republic of China, Washington, D.C.

In "Unearthing China's Past," an exhibition at the Museum of Fine Arts in 1973, one entire section was devoted to a group of well-known masterpieces of Chinese scroll painting and calligraphy, largely from the Museum's collection. These were shown with photographs of archaeological finds that shed new light on old problems concerning date, style, and origin of these famous handscrolls. The process has been almost reversed, however, in the present exhibition: copies of excavated wall paintings, drawn to exact scale, stand at the center of our attention as works of art and as invaluable sources of information on the daily life of China during the Han and T'ang periods. That they are also landmarks that may help us in dating and judging those few early paintings on paper and silk that have survived the ravages of time above ground is here of secondary importance.

The inspiration for this exhibition was a friendly gesture of a Japanese colleague, Professor Toh Sugimura: the gift of a catalogue of the exhibition "Wall Paintings from the Han and T'ang Periods from the People's Republic of China," held to celebrate the opening of the new municipal museum at Kita-Kyūshū, Japan, in the winter of 1974. During the intervening months, a great deal of preparation has been required to bring the exhibition to this country. The Museum is most grateful for the help and encouragement given by officials of the Liaison Office of the People's Republic of China in Washington, who relayed our ideas and requests to the proper authorities in Peking.

The present exhibition contains the same material as was shown in Japan, reproducing tomb paintings discovered in ten sites scattered all over Northern China and ranging in date from the early years of our era to the first decade of the eighth century. Although they represent only a small part of the actual finds, they convey an excellent impression of the diversity in style and subject matter, as well as of the colorful and monumental qualities of the originals.

In China the copying of works of art is an integral part of a long cultural tradition. Copies are not viewed there with the disdain so often reserved for them in the twentieth-century Western world. It is not surprising, therefore, that in a country where artists take an active part in all cultural activities on behalf of the larger public, painters of considerable talent and skill have placed themselves at the disposal of the archaeological services to make these copies. A careful comparison of the photographs of copies with photographic reproductions of the originals shows that the artists' effort has been, on the whole, one of painstaking accuracy. In the few instances where this did not seem to be the case, the discrepancies have been noted.

These copies of historic paintings are important for two reasons. The number of Americans who will be able to view the original murals *in situ* is minimal. It is only through reproductions such as these that the creations of artists who decorated ancient Chinese tombs can be made accessible to a larger public. Also, the exhibition of these copies offers a unique opportunity to place murals of different tombs in juxtaposition. The copies derive additional importance from the fact that some of the originals they represent have begun to deteriorate under the impact of changes, brought about by excavation, in the stable environment in which they have survived the centuries. Often made shortly after the discovery of the tomb, the copies are a permanent record of the condition of these paintings at the time they were unearthed.

The present catalogue is based, for the most part, on accounts of archaeologists and comments of Chinese scholars that have been published in Chinese archaeological journals. The authors of the catalogue have tried their utmost to do justice to the wealth of interesting observations made on these wall paintings by their Chinese colleagues, without whose many detailed studies this one could not have been written. Having seen neither originals nor copies prior to press time, the authors ask the reader's indulgence for any mistaken interpretation that may result from reliance on small reproductions and photographs alone. Occasionally they have ventured beyond what they found in Chinese publications, and it is hoped that the new interpretations presented in some of the entries will help to initiate a dialogue with Chinese colleagues. As much of their work is done in teams, the identity of those whom we should thank for contributions to the scholarship on these murals is not always known, but names have been mentioned in the Bibliography whenever possible.

Beyond acknowledging a great indebtedness to the Chinese, I would be remiss not to mention two American scholars whose works have helped me personally to gain a better understanding of the wall paintings and the culture they reflect. The perusal of Edward H. Schafer's *Golden Peaches of Samarkand,* a pleasure in itself, is an ideal preparation for anyone who wishes to taste the flavor of T'ang wall painting. The late William R. B. Acker's *T'ang and Pre-T'ang Texts on Chinese Painting* represents a scholar's work of a lifetime. His translations of ancient Chinese texts, of which I had the pleasure of editing the first part more than twenty years ago, seemed at that time a rather academic exercise. Recent findings of Chinese archaeologists have made it an invaluable source of information on this newly rediscovered art form that is in every respect as beautiful as the ancient chroniclers claimed.

JAN FONTEIN
Acting Director and Curator
of the Department of Asiatic Art
Museum of Fine Arts, Boston

Introduction

THERE are few aspects of ancient Chinese art on which the archaeologists of the People's Republic of China have been able to shed more new light than on the early history of Chinese painting. In the course of the continuing succession of spectacular finds that has made their achievement of the last twenty-five years one of the world's great adventures of archaeological discovery, Chinese archaeologists have succeeded in locating and opening a considerable number of brick and stone tombs, the walls of which are covered with paintings. As the number of the archaeological sites increased and the regional spread and chronological span of the finds widened, many new characteristics of the evolution of Chinese painting from the Western Han through the T'ang period gradually became evident, enabling scholars to reconstruct tentative outlines of the early history of an art form that many had long believed to be lost forever.

For the traditional Chinese connoisseur the art of Chinese painting consisted primarily of works on silk or paper. Although wall paintings in palaces and temples are frequently mentioned in ancient Chinese literature, references to wall paintings in tombs are rare. Moreover, if the existence of such murals was known at all, knowledge about them could hardly have spread far beyond the circles of grave robbers, who consistently ignored them. Although at one time, especially during the nineteen-thirties and -forties, Western scholars occupied themselves with the study of the Yüan and Ming murals in several major museums in Canada and the United States, it would seem that the younger generation of Western scholars shares the prejudice of the literati, whose works they admire so much, and that murals have hardly entered their sphere of interest.

Although the Italian word "fresco" is sometimes loosely used to describe murals, most Chinese wall paintings are executed in ink and mineral colors on dry plaster walls and are, therefore, different from true fresco, with which they cannot compete in durability. But it was not just natural fragility that caused the disappearance of almost all early examples of Chinese paintings, works on silk and paper as well as murals. In his *Record of Famous Painters of Successive Dynasties (Li-tai ming-hua chi)* the art historian Chang Yen-yüan (middle ninth century A.D.) described at length the tragic circumstances under which many of China's great art collections were dispersed and destroyed. The imperial tradition of collecting masterpieces of painting and calligraphy tended to concentrate the choicest examples of early Chinese painting in the imperial palace, where they were left exposed to all the dangers attendant to political upheavals. The inevitable result has been that very few examples of early Chinese painting have survived into modern times. Chang Yen-yüan, who lived to witness during the Hui-ch'ang era (A.D. 841-846) the total destruction of all the wall paintings in the Buddhist and Taoist monasteries of the two capitals of the T'ang empire that he himself had so painstakingly catalogued, must have had this tragic experience in mind when he lamented: "Now gold comes from the mountains, and pearls are produced in the waters and men gather these things without ceasing for all under Heaven to use. But paintings with the passage of months and years are destroyed and scattered until almost none are left. And since the famous men and ingenious scholars [who created them] can never live again, can one refrain from grief?" (Acker, vol. 1, pp. 209-10).

In contrast with the scarcity of extant early works of art is the wealth of information on early Chinese painting that has been preserved in literary sources. The importance of this documentary evidence had been realized in the West as early as 1897 when the enlightened sinologue Friedrich Hirth wrote *Native Sources of the History of Chinese Pictorial Art*. Only in recent decades, however, have scholars begun to translate literary works in which the early phases of Chinese painting are discussed and analyzed; at this time the majority of the basic treatises on painting have been printed in Western languages. Although they give us a wealth of often picturesque biographical information on the artists whose vanished masterpieces are recorded and praised, and a considerable amount of iconographical information can be gleaned from these sources, it is rather difficult to correlate the extensive information in the texts, especially that concerning style, with the scant visual evidence of early works of art. These discussions were doomed to revolve, therefore, again and again, around a small number of well-known works of art, in which some of the stylistic phenomena to which the texts alluded could actually be observed.

Perhaps underestimating the limitations naturally imposed on that medium, Osvald Sirén considered stone reliefs and engravings from Han offering shrines in Shantung "more or less faithful copies" of vanished paintings (Sirén, *Early Chinese Painting*, p. 6). Edouard Chavannes even went one step further and saw the lack of color in stone reliefs as the main feature that set reliefs and paintings apart (Chavannes, *Mission archéologique*, vol. 1, pp. 33-34). Assuming, moreover, that the reliefs were originally polychromed, he was inclined

to dismiss even this difference as one of no consequence.

There can be no doubt that some of the fundamental characteristics of Han painting have been preserved in reliefs and stone engravings, notably in its iconographic repertoire and in the methods of rendering space. There is an abundance of literary evidence for the assumption that themes represented by painters on the walls of palaces and other official buildings were in many respects the same as those on the walls of tombs. The officials who make their appearance in the murals of the tomb at Wang-tu (nos. 6-12) are the same police officers, comptrollers, and other minor bureaucrats who parade in their chariots on the stone walls of the offering houses, each of them clearly identified by labels. The story of "Killing Three Warriors with Two Peaches" on the painted lintel of the Western Han tomb at Lo-yang has its counterpart at the Wu-liang offering shrine as well as in a mortuary relief at Nan-yang. The composition of the bridge scenes in murals of the tomb at Holingol (see no. 15) is exactly paralleled in several reliefs from Shantung and Kiangsu. It would be easy to multiply examples demonstrating the close ties that existed between painting and relief sculpture during the Han period. Yet it would seem that Chavannes placed too much emphasis on iconography and overlooked the basic differences between the two media, chisel and stone, on the one hand, and brush and plaster, on the other.

The Western scholar who was perhaps the first to make this distinction clearly was Otto Fischer. His pioneering study *Die chinesische Malerei der Han-Dynastie* (1931) deals with this complex problem in a manner that does justice to the stylistic and artistic implications of it. Fischer was also the first to understand the great importance of the painted lintel and pediment of a tomb in the Museum of Fine Arts in Boston, that he—quite correctly, as later archaeological excavations would prove—attributed to the Han dynasty in spite of the almost unanimous opinion of other Western scholars, who assigned it to a later period (reproduced in Fontein and Wu, *Unearthing China's Past*, pp. 96 and 97). As a result of the extensive

 No. 15, from an Eastern Han tomb near Holingol, Inner Mongolia (see p. 38)

11 No. 113, from the T'ang tomb of Li Hsien (see p. 94)

excavations carried out by Chinese archaeologists in the area around Lo-yang in recent years, we know now how rarely the find of a lintel and pediment comparable to the Boston tiles occurs; only two other tombs with similar detachable and painted tiles have been discovered among the hundreds of Han tombs in that area.

Perhaps because the figure scenes on the Boston lintel are related both in composition and in content to those of an early handscroll now in the British Museum, *Admonitions of the Court Instructress,* attributed to the fourth-century painter Ku K'ai-chih, these two lone survivors of early Chinese painting present to the art historian a deceptively consistent image. Emphasis on continuity in pictorial tradition makes us almost lose sight of the fact that among the countless works of art that had been lost many could have represented divergent styles that did not fit as perfectly in our framework of ideas as do the Boston tiles and the *Admonitions.* How many centuries separate these two landmarks of early Chinese painting is unclear, for the *Admonitions of the Court Instructress,* like the few other surviving early masterpieces, confronts the art historian with two distinct problems: one concerns the date of the style to which a work appears to conform, and the other is the actual date that the work was executed.

In order to solve this twofold problem a comparison with datable material of unquestionable authenticity is indispensable. For many years, the only early pictorial material for which a date could be established beyond reasonable doubt was that preserved in the imperial storehouse Shōsōin at Nara, Japan, where the furniture and personal belongings of the Emperor Shōmu were deposited in the middle of the eighth century. Although the date of this collection is firmly established, there is a disadvantage in that its provenance (Chinese, Japanese, or perhaps even Korean) is often unclear.

To this has been added the material that came to light in the first phase of archaeological exploration in China, during the occupation of China's northeastern provinces by the Japanese. At that time several Han tombs containing wall paintings were excavated in Liao-ning Province, near Liao-yang, at Ying-ch'eng-tzu (near the present Lü-ta), and in what was once the kingdom of Koguryŏ in Chi-an County, along the Yalu River. Moreover, Japanese archaeologists discovered many wall paintings in Han tombs in the vicinity of Pyŏng-yang (North Korea). Although the significance of all these finds was certainly not lost on Japanese scholars, Western historians have tended to view the murals found in these tombs with reservations. Their provenance was, of course, firmly established, and their early date, even if not always specific, beyond question; however, the artistic quality of the murals failed to arouse enthusiasm. First of all, the murals were considered to be products of a tradition of mortuary craftsmanship with commissions executed from a stock repertory, an art form that could in no way compare with creations of superior individualistic artists who are eulogized in literary sources, Also, these early examples of Chinese and Korean wall painting were viewed primarily as the work of provincial schools, flourishing on the periphery of a great vanished metropolitan culture much discussed in Chinese literature, but lacking any surviving examples to document it. In this respect they were considered to fall into the same category as the thousands of Buddhist wall paintings found in the gigantic cave temple complex at Tun-huang (Kansu Province) in the northwest of China. Although points of correspondence between the Buddhist murals and the wall paintings of the temples of the two T'ang capitals, as described in Chang Yen-yüan's *Record of Famous Painters of Successive Dynasties* (see p. 9), were too numerous to be ignored, the general feeling prevailed that these provincial paintings could convey only an imperfect impression of a much more sophisticated metropolitan style.

Twenty-five years of archaeological exploration and discovery in the People's Republic of China have uncovered such an overwhelming amount of information on early Chinese painting that many opinions based upon the study of material long available to us should be reappraised in the light of new archaeological evidence. It has been pointed out that in the short history of the study of Chinese art in the West, large and important exhibitions have often succeeded in opening the eyes of scholars and in changing the direction and emphasis of their research. The spectacular traveling exhibitions from the People's Republic of China have only recently returned to Peking and it is therefore perhaps too early to begin to assess the kind of impact they may have had on the scholarly world in addition to their extraordinarily widespread popular appeal. Judging from recent publications, one would think that they have not yet brought about a reorientation of our scholarly research, most of which is still conducted within the narrow confines of familiar material from Tun-huang, the Shōsōin, and the burned murals of the Hōryūji. It is hoped that with this exhibition, the attention of Western students of early Chinese painting can be directed toward an inexhaustible source of visual data provided by the newly discovered murals and that this will expand their horizons beyond the territory thoroughly investigated in the past.

For the Chinese archaeologists the first priority would seem to be the recording of excavations and the preservation of tombs and their rich contents. In view of the frequency with which new and exciting discoveries are being made, these tasks alone place a great burden on the Chinese. What Western art historical research can contribute is not yet clear; the inaccessibility of the actual murals is bound to remain a formidable obstacle to original research and obviously places strict limitations on what we can and should do. It would be far beyond the competence of the authors of this catalogue, and it would clearly exceed the scope of this project, if we were to make a first attempt, here, at a critical appraisal, analysis, and synthesis of the problems posed by the murals. Yet it is possible to offer a few observations that may help to place some of these questions in a somewhat different perspective.

The wall paintings of which copies and photographic reproductions are shown in this exhibition, as well as the many murals that have been discovered in other Chinese tombs, can be studied from several points of view. To the archaeologist and the historian the murals represent, first and foremost, a unique repository of visual information on a great variety of cultural and social phenomena. They embody a unique pictorial record of the material culture and social organization of the Chinese empire from the Han through the T'ang dynasty. The extensive archaeological literature that has appeared in China during the last twenty-five years shows that Chinese historians, with their incomparable command of China's classical literature and their peerless heuristic skills, are masters at matching visual evidence unearthed in archaeological excavations with the literary evidence of ancient Chinese records, which often explain or identify an object found in a tomb or depicted in the murals on its walls. The epigraphic finds in tombs are of particular interest because they constitute independent proof, unaltered by the faulty transmission that so often has made written historical records unreliable. Excavations have provided a wealth of solid new information on geographical names, official titles, social structure, and ritual, the cumulative effect of which is of inestimable value to a critical reappraisal of textual sources. More important, perhaps, is the extraordinarily vivid depiction in these murals of phenomena that are described at great length in the annals, such as the Chinese dealings with their northern neighbors, or other aspects of Chinese history, for example, the lifestyles of different social classes.

Ancient Chinese society had a carefully stratified hierarchy of officialdom organized in a huge pyramidal structure dominated by the emperor, who was supposed to rule by mandate from Heaven. The material privileges and status symbols accorded to mandarins of each rank in the hierarchy were established by law. A variety of telling details in the murals prove that this elaborate hierarchical system followed those who were part of the official machinery into their graves. The murals in the Han tombs at Wang-tu and Holingol, as well as those of all four T'ang tombs represented in this exhibition, contain numerous visual references to these hierarchical distinctions. For just as the artists of the murals, in re-creating the life of the deceased, would not have considered showing the entourage in costumes that were *démodé* at the time of the funeral, it was equally unlikely that they would have shown the occupant without the number of bodyguards or escorts commensurate with his official status, or without the paraphernalia to which he was entitled by law.

Matching of visual data with text references can work both ways, for not only can a passage in a text elucidate a picture, but a line of verse or prose describing or alluding to a specific object or situation can suddenly acquire new meaning when seen in conjunction with a painted image of the same theme. The wealth and diversity of China's literary heritage is so great that historians, by systematically collecting information from the entire range of Chinese literature, often succeed in re-creating an image of an era or of a historical or social phenomenon. Edward H. Schafer's study of T'ang exotics, *Golden Peaches of Samarkand,* is one of the most brilliant and imaginative works in this genre that Western sinology has produced. It contains essays on so many of the customs and costumes, games, and pastimes illustrated in the wall paintings found in T'ang tombs that our appreciation of them acquires a new dimension when viewed with Schafer's study as a guide.

Han tombs date from a period in which it was not yet customary to deposit a tombstone, inscribed with a biography of the deceased, in or near the mortuary chamber and, as a consequence, the exact date of the early tombs is often difficult to establish. During the T'ang period, however, tombstones were in general use, with the result that many of the excavated T'ang tombs can be dated almost exactly. At least six tombs containing seventh-century wall paintings have been preserved, while the first dozen years of the eighth century yielded an equal number of tombs. The economic decline brought about by the rebellion of An Lu-shan during the middle of the eighth century made many abandon

14 No. 118, from the T'ang tomb of Li Hsien (see p. 97)

15 No. 122, from the T'ang tomb of Li Hsien (see p. 101)

the tradition of lavish burials and very few tombs decorated with murals date from after that time.

The fact that so many of the excavated T'ang tombs can be dated by the mortuary inscription of the deceased who was buried there enables us to study particular phenomena in considerable chronological detail. The critic Yao Tsui, speaking, in his *Hsü Hua-p'in,* of practical problems that Chinese painters face, mentions the rapidity of change in fashions: "Add to this the fact that in recent times the make-up and the costumes have changed [as often as] three times in one month, so that before one can make head or tail of them, they have suddenly gone out of style" (Acker, vol. 1, pp. 37-38). Of the famous painter and art theoretician Hsieh Ho the same author writes: "[Even] the festive robes and the cosmetics of his women changed according to the times and he made straight eyebrows or curved forehead locks according to the latest [fashion] in the world's affairs" (Acker, vol. 1, p. 46).

Although Yao Tsui's claim of three changes in fashion per month is perhaps to be considered a poetic exaggeration, the extraordinarily large number of exactly datable tombs excavated during the last twenty-five years permits us to make an accurate and detailed chronology of the changes in fashion in China during the period of the Northern and Southern dynasties and the Sui and T'ang periods. A firm chronological framework could be established by the large quantity of dated tomb figurines; however, the much rarer wall paintings provide extremely helpful details that would remain unnoticed if we had to rely on figurines alone. Comparison of these two art forms makes evident that they were created in the same spirit and that they portray the same customs, activities, and fashions. The women depicted in murals of the tomb of Princess Yung-t'ai (see no. 141) have an exact counterpart in tomb figurines found in nearby graves of her close relatives (see nos. 137 and 138), and the mounted huntsmen with their cheetahs that parade *in effigie* on the wall of the passageway in Li Hsien's tomb (see nos. 108-12) are identical with pottery figurines from Yung-t'ai's tomb (see Watson, *Chinese Exhibition,* p. 139, fig. 275). This close resemblance between two art forms existed to some extent in Han times, but reached its apogee during the T'ang dynasty. It brings to mind biographical information concerning the T'ang painter Yang Hui-chih. He and the famous painter Wu Tao-tzu together studied the work of the artist Chang Seng-yu. When Yang saw that he would never equal the skill of his colleagues he burned his brushes and devoted himself solely to sculpting. According to a saying of the time, Wu's painting and Yang's modeling had both captured Chang's divine brush method.

APART from the importance of tomb murals as a source of visual information on the material and social culture of the periods during which they were made, the art-historical information they yield is of enormous interest. The first point to be established is whether the murals in tombs reflect accurately highly developed styles of painting described and recorded in Chinese literary sources. It is necessary, therefore, to consider whether the old objections that these paintings are either provincial or of funerary (i.e., inferior) quality are still valid. With the exception of Holingol in the Autonomous Region of Inner Mongolia and Chia-yü-kuan in Kansu Province, the tomb sites represented in this exhibition are all in the real heartland of Chinese culture. Moreover, the Han tomb at Lo-yang and all of the T'ang tombs shown here can be said to be examples of typical metropolitan styles. Whatever our judgment of the originals of the murals will be, the argument that they are the artistic creations of provincial schools does not, therefore, apply to them. The question remains whether the murals may be considered works of somewhat inferior quality by virtue of the circumstance that they were discovered in tombs. There is considerable literary evidence that the repertoire of iconographic themes encountered in Han tombs is in many respects the same as that of murals in palaces and official buildings, but since the latter have not survived, we have, of course, no reliable information as to whether there was a marked difference in the quality of execution.

For the T'ang period the situation is somewhat different. Tombs in sections VII through X in this exhibition once housed the mortal remains of members of the Li family, the ruling clan of the T'ang dynasty. At least two of them appear not to have died a natural death. They may have committed suicide or may have been put to death at the command of the Empress Wu Tse-t'ien. Immediately after the death of this empress, the only woman ever to attain the status of ruling monarch in the entire dynastic history of China, a combination of traditionalist prejudice and anti-feminist bias set the stage for the bad press that she has had throughout Chinese history. Her political, administrative, and cultural achievements received little mention in official chronicles, as the dynastic historians focused on events at court, with its endless intrigues, rather than on developments in the country at large. As a consequence, we have more gossip about her private life and her allegedly questionable morals than about her skills and achievements.

Whatever the cause of death of the relatives of Empress Wu—and in the case of Princess Yung-t'ai (see no. 141) there are strong indications that the official dynastic history does not tell us the truth—it is of interest to note that these are not ordinary burials, but reburials carried out after the empress died. The elevated status of all these members of the imperial house entitled them to the most lavish entombment, and if any injustice had been done the emperor and his court officials would have had all the more reason to make these funerals, even by imperial T'ang standards, extraordinarily opulent. We may be confident that the wall paintings are the best that China could create at the time these tombs were constructed and that they are not in any way a form of inferior funerary art.

Another vital clue concerning the superior quality of T'ang tomb paintings comes with the discovery that those in the tomb of Li Chung-jun (see p. 104) are the work of the artist Yang Pien [-lu?], whose name occurs mistakenly as Ch'ang Pien in the late Ming edition of Chang Yen-yüan's *Record of Famous Painters of Successive Dynasties* (illustrated in Wang Jên-p'o, *Kaogu,* 1973, no. 6, p. 381, fig. 1). It establishes for the first time a clear connection between the murals in the tombs and the artists whose names were considered worthy of inclusion in that famous art historical document. For many years the study of early Chinese painting consisted of the analysis of literary sources such as this and material of a more anecdotal character, in an effort to extract ideas about the techniques and styles of ancient masters. This approach has made us resigned to the fact that the great works of art have been irretrievably lost. Now we may have to become accustomed to the idea that some of them have survived. In all probability the handscrolls were lost in the political upheavals that cost the emperors of T'ang, Southern T'ang, and Northern Sung their prized collections of paintings. Also lost, by Sung times, were the few wall paintings that were spared during the anti-Buddhist and anti-Taoist measures of the Hui-ch'ang era, but it is in the murals of the imperial tombs that some of the work has indeed survived.

Chinese connoisseurs and art critics have often resorted to metaphor in order to describe artistic and stylistic phenomena. For this reason, even such a detailed study as Chang Yen-yüan's *Record of Famous Painters of Successive Dynasties,* which has been cited in this catalogue over and again, does not always describe what we see in the murals as precisely as factual information in tomb inscriptions tends to match statements in recorded history. Yet, reading through Chang Yen-yüan's text, one is constantly reminded of the visual impressions generated by the wall paintings. For example, the vigor and firmness of brushwork in the murals in Li Shou's tomb (see p. 78) is immediately brought to mind by Chang Yen-yüan's famous description of the brush technique of the great Wu Tao-tzu: "... so he bent his bows, brandished his swords, planted his pillars and placed his beams without resorting to line-brush or ruler ..." (Acker, vol. 1, p. 180). And the biography of Han Kan, the great horse painter, with its vivid description of famous horses and the stylistic changes that took place in their portrayal by masters of the past, can be fully appreciated only when we see horses of many different breeds, painted in so many different styles, adorning the walls of the tombs.

WHEN we attempt to sum up how and in what respect murals discovered during the last twenty-five years have helped to advance our knowledge of early Chinese painting, the following points would seem to stand out as most important. The number of landscape paintings on silk and paper traditionally thought to represent the styles of the T'ang and pre-T'ang periods is extremely small. Even in Northern Sung times their number seems to have been minimal, if we can believe such astute connoisseurs as Mi Fu (1052-1106). The study of these few isolated survivors of a great tradition is hampered by the fact that the actual date of execution is often quite different from that suggested by the style in which they have been painted (even if their authenticity has not been challenged, as is sometimes the case). The murals, on the other hand, constitute a body of material of unquestionable authenticity. As the date of the execution and that of the style is obviously the same, they provide reliable information on technique, style, and iconography of the period that may help to evaluate other paintings that have been the subject of modern scholarly inquiry for many years.

This critical canon is more useful still with regard to figure painting. Since the Northern Sung period, when figure painting ceded its position of preeminence to landscape painting, Chinese connoisseurs have had to rely on copies to recapture the spirit of the early, glorious phase of this art form. Repeated copying, in the course of which later stylistic mannerisms and concepts crept into the original composition, has in some cases changed the appearance of the old masterpieces. Copies of Wang Hsi-chih's calligraphic work *Preface to the Gathering at the Orchid Pavilion* (written in A.D. 353)

18 No. 135, from the T'ang tomb of Li Chung-jun (see p. 114)

19 No. 141, from the T'ang tomb of Hsien-hui (see p. 123)

are a well-known example: their reliability has been brought into question by the discovery of a different calligraphic style on tombstones of members of the artist's family (see Fontein and Wu, *Unearthing China's Past*, pp. 210-12). Likewise, the discovery of murals and that of the lacquered screen in the tomb of Ssŭ-ma Chin-lung (died A.D. 484; see *Wen Wu*, 1972, no. 8, pp. 55-60) makes it possible to establish the accuracy with which Chinese painters have transmitted styles of some of the most celebrated artists of the past, such as Ku K'ai-chih and Yen Li-pen.

Although it is certainly too early to assess completely the results of this confrontation between hallowed tradition and archaeological fact, it would seem, at first glance, that the transmission of the old masters has been more accurate than we have sometimes been inclined to believe. For example, it has long been thought that illusionistic shading to achieve an effect of volume was entirely a practice of foreign origin, imported into China along with the techniques and iconography of Buddhism. The visual evidence of the murals leaves no doubt of the fact that shading antedates the importation of Buddhist painting techniques; it is already visible, in rudimentary form, in some of the Han murals. The *ts'un*, or surface texture strokes, that give substance and volume to rocks and mountains in later T'ang paintings seem to have evolved gradually from the use of washes and shading that were current in earlier periods. The often expressed opinion that the *Admonitions of the Court Instructress*, attributed to Ku K'ai-chih (see p. 12), betrays its later date by the shading technique applied to the costumes would seem to stand corrected by irrefutable visual evidence of the murals.

The regional spread of the sites in which wall paintings have been discovered provides an opportunity to reevaluate the question of so-called provincial styles. Unlike the vast numbers of mortuary objects that have been found all over China, making it possible to recognize many regional styles and types of art, the number of murals is perhaps not yet large enough to study this problem with the same degree of accuracy as can be done in the fields of ceramics or bronzes. However, judging from material that has come to light so far, it would seem that actual stylistic differences between metropolitan styles and those of the provinces and border regions are not as evident as previously thought, but it appears that there are, within all periods, unquestionable differences in artistic quality.

Although the present exhibition consists of copies and photographic reproductions, it does justice to the originals in more than one respect. In Chang Yen-yüan's *Record of Famous Painters of Successive Dynasties* it is said: "in the old days people used to be fond of making tracings of paintings. They would succeed seven or eight times out of ten without missing the general atmosphere [of the subject] or the [individual] brush strokes" (Acker, vol. 1, p. 191). The copies presented in this exhibition demonstrate that Chinese painters of today are in this respect no less skilled than their distant forebears. For although it is sometimes difficult to reproduce the artistic tension of a calligraphic line, the copies do give an accurate impression of style, composition, dimensions, and color. They have re-created for us the spirit of vitality and freshness of observation with which artists of the past depicted on the walls of tombs the lifestyles and customs of various ethnic groups.

JAN FONTEIN

I

Western Han Tomb No. 61 near Lo-yang, Honan Province

During the second half of 1957 a team of archaeologists of the Bureau of Culture, Honan Province, excavated a Western Han tomb located about one kilometer from the northwest corner of Old Lo-yang, about halfway between the ancient city and the Shao-kou cemetery, excavated a few years earlier. The tomb was moved to the Wang-ch'eng Park in Lo-yang, where it is accessible to the public.

The structure consists of a large (eighteen feet long) main chamber with a gate opening on the east, two lateral chambers extending toward the north and south, and two smaller side chambers projecting from the larger ones in an easterly direction. The main chamber is divided by a lintel and a pediment consisting of three hollow tiles, supported in the middle by a single hollow column. The walls, the roof (trapezoidal in cross-section), and the floor of the main chamber are constructed with hollow tiles decorated with stamped designs, whereas the vaulted lateral chambers are of brick. A comparison with other tombs of similar structure and typological analysis of the tomb furniture indicate that this example dates from sometime during the last half of the first century B.C. or the first decades of the first century A.D.

The most striking feature of the tomb is the paintings of the main chamber. These are found on the square tile of the pediment over the inside of the gate; on both sides of the pediment and lintel of the partition and on their supporting column; on two panels, together forming a kind of architrave of trapezoidal shape, on the rear wall; and, finally, across twelve tiles of the ceiling. These constitute the earliest major example of Chinese wall painting and are, therefore, of unusual historical and artistic interest. Of the richly decorated, partially reticulated pediment and lintel no copies seem to have been made, all the more regrettable as this part of the tomb provides the first solid basis for comparison with the well-known Boston tiles, obviously taken from a tomb of the same type (see Fontein and Wu, *Unearthing China's Past*, pp. 96-100). One of the figure scenes on the lintel has been identified with certainty by the Chinese scholar Kuo Mo-jo as an illustration of the anecdote "Killing Three Warriors with Two Peaches" (for an English version, see George Kao, *Chinese Wit and Humor*, New York: Sterling Publishing Company, 1974, pp. 43-45).

The paintings are all done in fine, calligraphically modulated brushwork in ink with the addition of mineral colors such as vermilion, brown, yellow, green, and a kind of purplish ultramarine. The artist portrays almost grotesque figures in highly expressive postures and with exaggerated facial expressions. Only a few, as, for example, the two guards in the banquet scene, resemble the more solemn, dignified type of person to be found on the lintel of the Boston tiles.

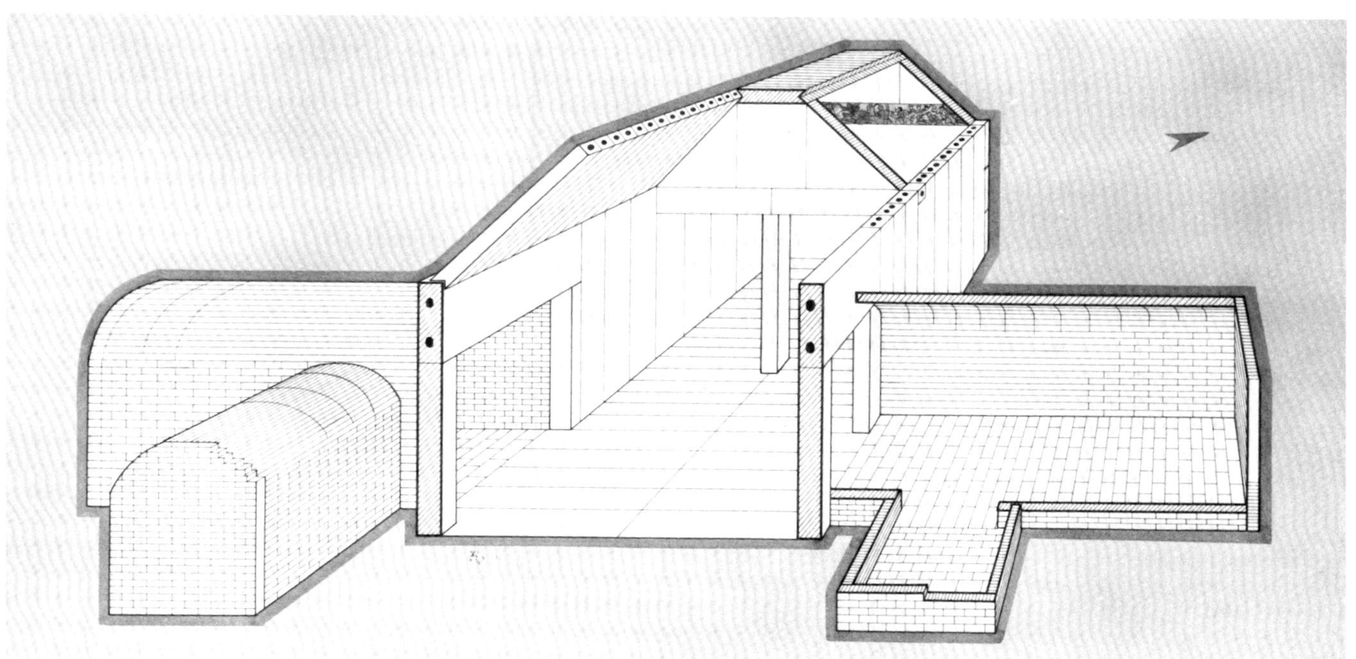

Entry numbers in this catalogue correspond with those in the Kita-Kyūshū catalogue (see Bibliography).

1

Constellations, sun, and moon

(ceiling of main chamber of tomb)

These cosmological elements are painted on twelve hollow tiles. At the far right is the sun, recognizable by its symbol, the black crow. The seventh tile from the right shows the moon, enclosing a rabbit and a frog. The other tiles all represent constellations, surrounded by stylized clouds. The moon is painted green, the sun and the stars red, and the clouds black—all against a white background.

The second tile from the right, the Northern Dipper (Ursa Major) or *Pei-tou,* is followed by nine of the twenty-eight "lunar mansions," i.e., equatorial divisions or segments of the celestial sphere bounded by hour circles. According to Joseph Needham, this system of "lunar mansions" (*hsiu*) foreshadowed the accurate division of the heavens into delineated constellation fields (Needham, *Science and Civilization in China,* pp. 234-38).

After an initial effort at identification by Li Ching-hua, a more detailed study by Hsia Nai ("Constellations") has established the identity of these "lunar mansions," with their determinative stars, as follows (right to left):

Fang ("room") with Pi Scorpii
Pi ("net") with Epsilon Tauri and
Mao (Pleiades) with Nu Tauri
Hsin ("heart") with Sigma Scorpii
Kuei ("ghost") with Theta Cancri
the moon
Hsü ("void") with Beta Aquarii and
Wei ("rooftop") with Alpha Aquarii
Ho Ku or *Chien Niu* ("herding boy") with Beta Capricorni
Chih Nü ("weaving girl") with Alpha Lyrae
Liu ("willow") with Delta Hydrae
Shen with Zeta Orionis

As the tomb was constructed on an east-west axis, the twelve ceiling tiles with the cosmological paintings are lined up along the same axis, placing the sun in the east at the entrance. Thus the macrocosm of the universe and the decoration of the tomb were brought into complete harmony.

2

Banquet at Hung-Men [?]

(tile architrave on rear wall of main chamber)

This scene has been tentatively identified as the so-called Banquet at Hung-men, a historic event that took place in 206 B.C. during the final struggle for supremacy between Hsiang Yü and Liu Pang after the fall of the Ch'in dynasty and shortly before Liu Pang ascended the throne as the first Han emperor Kao-tsu. On the right two servants are preparing meat, which one of them barbecues over a flaming stove; large pieces of meat are suspended on hooks above them. The head of a cow appears incongruously between the undulating mountains, as if it were part of the display of meat. This may have led Kuo Mo-jo to suggest that the mountains do not represent an actual landscape setting, but a "mural within a mural" (see *Wen Wu Ching-hua,* no. 3, pp. 27-29).

The next two men are presumably the rivals Hsiang Yü, holding a drinking horn, and Liu Pang, looking back almost apprehensively over his shoulder at Hsiang Yü. To their left stands a third man, Hsiang Po, who had placed himself betwen Liu Pang and the fierce-looking sword dancer Hsiang Chuang on the extreme left, who intended to assassinate Liu Pang. Hsiang Chuang is accompanied by two figures resembling the guards in the Boston tiles (see fig. 1; Museum of Fine Arts, Boston, 25.10).

The hairy monster steated cross-legged in the center is dressed in a long-sleeved robe. Like the figure identified as Hsiang Yü, he holds a drinking horn, suggesting that he is a participant in the banquet. Kuo Mo-jo, aware of the absence of any supernatural demonic being from the Banquet story, presumes that it is merely a painted representation, resembling tigers painted on a gate outside a royal audience hall. The explanation of the most conspicuous feature of the entire scene as part of the background decoration does not seem entirely satisfactory, but no other valid suggestion has been made.

2

detail, 2

Fig. 1

II

Eastern Han Tomb at P'ing-lu, Shansi Province

In April 1959, a Han tomb decorated with wall paintings was discovered at Tsao-yüan-ts'un, P'ing-lu County, Shansi Province. The county cultural office had the tomb excavated during the following two months and commemorated the successful conclusion of this undertaking by organizing a local exhibition of the finds.

The tomb is of brick, vaulted and with an opening on the east side. The main chamber measures about fourteen by seven feet and is six and one-half feet high. A small side chamber is attached on the south side. Although at one time the entire tomb must have been covered with wall paintings, most of the paint has flaked; only those on the upper parts of the walls and the ceiling have been relatively well preserved. The bricks were covered with clay mixed with wheat chaff over which a finishing layer of whitewash was applied. Ink and colors (red, yellow, indigo, and blue), used in varying shades, were applied directly to this finishing coat.

The decoration consists of murals dealing with two themes. One is that of the Four Directional Animals, three of which are clearly discernible in their appropriate place on the ceiling: the Azure Dragon (east), the White Tiger (west), and the Dark Warrior, i.e., the Tortoise and Serpent (north). These paintings are reproduced in the excavation report (*Kaogu*, 1959, no. 9, pp. 462-63 [pl. 1]), but no copies of them have been made. The landscapes and farming scenes that constitute the other part of the repertoire have been described below.

3

Mountain landscape with architecture

(east end of top register of north wall)

This partial copy depicts a compound at the foot of the mountains. The building is U-shaped and identified by the authors of *Murals from the Han to the T'ang Dynasty* as a fortified house, but it is difficult to interpret the details from the photograph of a copy.

Most of the space is taken up by four mountain ranges (about one third of those shown in the original), the contours of which are indicated in rather thick black lines. For such an early example of landscape painting the spatial arrangement is quite sophisticated. The placement of trees along the outlines of the undulating mountains is reminiscent of paintings of a much later date, such as *The Nymph of the Lo River* in the Freer Gallery, a Sung painting in the manner of Ku K'ai-chih (active ca. A.D. 400). Clouds and a white bird resembling a heron have been used effectively to suggest space and depth. A large section immediately to the left of this scene is reproduced in no. 4.

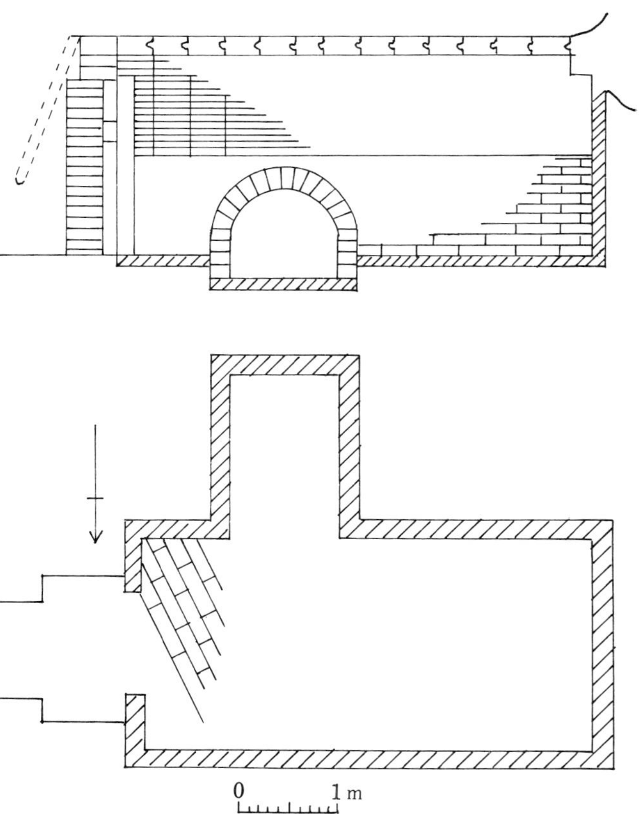

4

4 *See also color plate, p. 6.*
Landscape with farmers at work
(east end of top register of north wall)

In the lower left a farmer wearing a hat is squatting under a tree holding a stick between his legs. Behind him a basket (or cage) hangs from the tree. To the right we see a sketchily drawn scene of a farmer working in his field with a three-legged, ox-drawn seeder. In the center foreground is another ink sketch of a farmer carrying two baskets on a pole. Directly above him, across the stream (indicated by thin lines), are other farmers at work. One rides in a horse-drawn cart; another squats next to his buffalo in the stream. A highly stylized tree separates these two scenes. The mountains in the background are a continuation of those in no. 3. Clouds drawn in an archaizing style have been placed here and there in the composition for decorative effect. In the upper left corner is a small house on top of a hill, its open facade draped with curtains in typical Han fashion.

It is quite remarkable to see nature depicted in a poetic and sensitive manner at this early stage of Chinese landscape painting. The spatial arrangement of atmospheric elements, as well as the relationship between landscape and human activities, has been managed quite skillfully.

5
Plowing scene
(north end of west wall, just below Dark Warrior)

This partial copy is distinguished by a rather unusual composition (for the complete painting see *Kaogu,* 1959, no. 9, pl. 1). In the upper left corner is a small house, depicted in heavy blacks, with only a minimum of architectural detail; it is flanked by bare trees. In front of the house is, according to the excavation report, a wide open space painted in a pinkish color. Except for this color, it would be interpreted as part of the field below, where a farmer tilling the soil with an ox-drawn plow is shown. Of the farmer only the vaguest outlines are visible, and of the man dressed in a long black gown standing behind him (according to the excavation report) nothing is visible in the copy (see *Kaogu,* 1959, no. 9, p. 463).

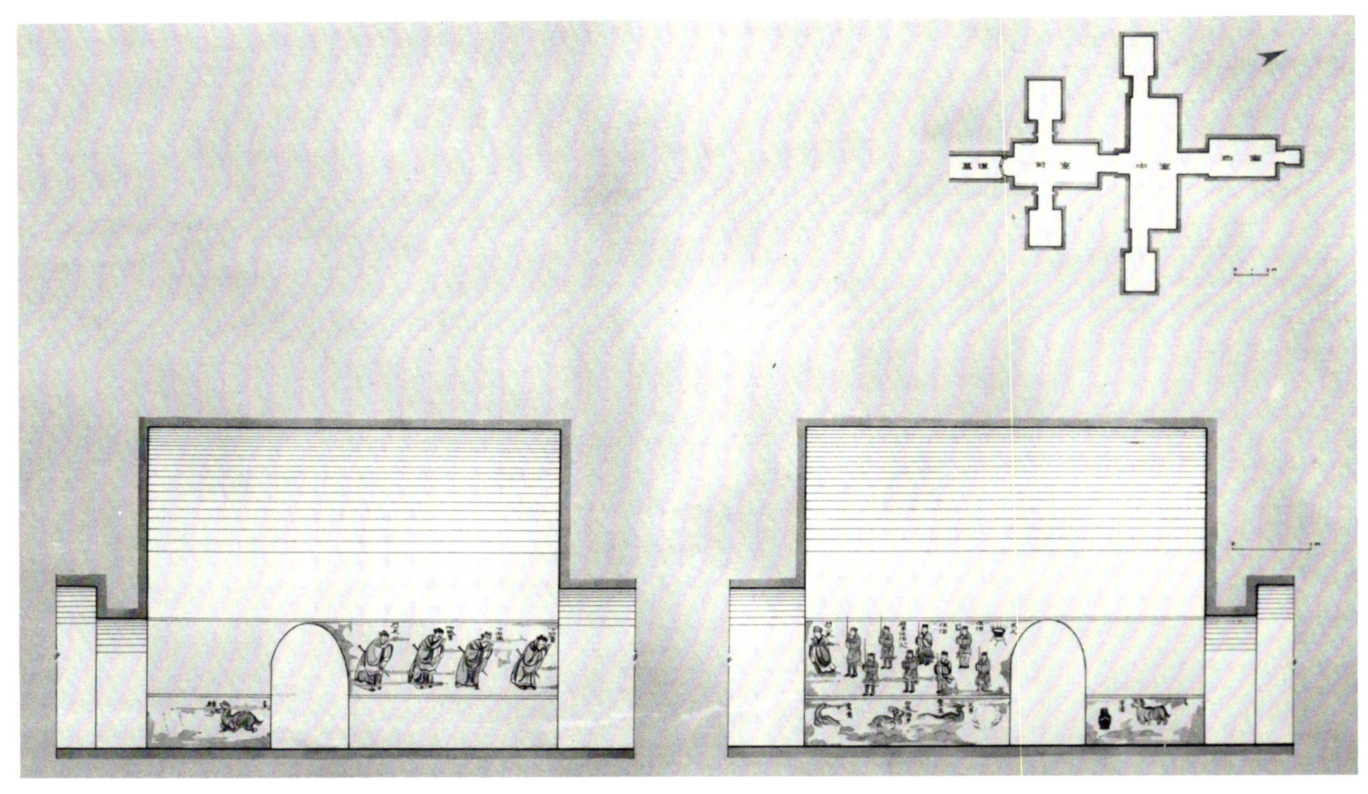

III

Eastern Han Tomb No. 1 at Wang-tu, Hopei Province

THIS tomb was excavated in March 1952 at So-yao-ts'un, Wang-tu County, Western Hopei. It was one of the first successes of the new archaeological services of the People's Republic of China, and to this date it remains one of the finest Han tombs to have been scientifically excavated. Another found in April 1955 in its immediate vicinity was assigned the number 2.

Tomb no. 1 is surmounted by a tumulus about thirty-three feet high. Built of a fine-quality brick, it consists of a passageway and three vaulted chambers of which the front and middle chamber each have two side chambers; the rear chamber has a smaller post-chamber at the back. All are connected by passageways, and the total length from the tomb entrance to the north wall of the post-chamber measures sixty feet.

The tomb had been robbed twice (a few mortuary objects were recovered), but most of the wall paintings, as well as the inscriptions, were found intact. Nearly all murals are located on the four walls of the front chamber. They consist of two registers separated by a horizontal line, with human figures in the upper part and animals and birds in the lower. All figures and animals are accompanied by brief inscriptions stating the title of the person portrayed or the name of the animal. According to these labels, the figures were all officials who served under the occupant of the tomb; the birds and animals are auspicious symbols.

The excavation report indicates that a thin layer of plaster was applied to the wall as a base on which ink and mineral colors (cinnabar, mineral blue, and yellow) were painted. Copies included in this exhibition represent wall paintings on the east, west, and north walls. They were made by staff members of the Historical Museum in Peking in June 1954.

An indication as to the date of the tomb can be found in a short inscription discovered in the corridor leading into the western side chamber of the front chamber. It was written in the form of an eight-line eulogy in rhyming verse, the literary genre associated with painting during the Han period. After extensive research and discussion, Chinese scholars generally seem to agree that the tomb is the burying place of a duke of Fou-yang of the Eastern Han period, but it is not certain which of the three persons who held this title in succession was buried here. In view of the fact that the second tomb at Wang-tu can be dated by its inscription to the year A.D. 182, it is likely that tomb no. 1 dates from approximately the same time.

6

Four officials

(upper register of west wall of front chamber)

The rank or function of the four officials depicted in this scene is indicated by inscriptions that accompany each. They are, from right to left: *Kung-ts'ao,* the Achievement Officer, in charge of promotions and demotions, rewards and fines; *Yu-chiao,* the Circuit Officer, in charge of inspection tours; *Tse-ts'ao,* the Thieves Officer, in charge of security; and *Men-hsia-shih,* the Administrative Officer. All four are shown leaning forward, holding their tablets of office in their hands, as if paying homage to the deceased. The painting technique, style, and iconography of these four figures are virtually alike, except for slight variations in the headgear, undoubtedly an indication of a difference in their duties. The ink tones and brushstrokes are surprisingly varied: outlines of the garments are drawn in

6

delicate lines, quite similar to the "iron-wire" lines of later periods. For draperies a bold, free style is used, reminiscent of the *p'o-mo* ("spilled ink") technique of later times. The wide garments, painted with heavy black lines along the folds of the draperies, give the figures an air of stability and seriousness; whether the heavy accents were meant as effects of shading is not entirely clear. The same technique translated into stone can be seen in the large Han tomb at I-nan (Shantung Province), in which the drapery folds of figures on the engraved stone slabs are sometimes accentuated by striations and hatching (as Laurence Sickman was the first to suggest; see Sickman and Soper, p. 293). If this is indeed shading, the same characteristics in later works such as, for example, the *Admonitions of the Court Instructress* attributed to Ku K'ai-chih (see p. 12) or *The Thirteen Emperors* attributed to Yen Li-pen (see p. 94) may well represent a further development of a Han technique instead of an imported novelty (see also p. 20).

In the chapter on equipages and costumes (*Yü-fu-chih*) in the *History of the Later Han Dynasty,* it is said that officials in charge of security are customarily equipped with long swords, and this illustration confirms the statement. A closer inspection of photographs of the original wall paintings reveals that the sword guards are painted in a bright mineral green, suggesting that they may have been carved from jade. The hilts appear to be wound with rope like the silk cord wound around hilts of swords found in tombs of the period.

7-9
Animal and bird frieze

(nos. 7 and 8: lower register of walls of front chamber just inside entry; no. 9: lower register of north end of east wall of front chamber)

According to the label, the animal in no. 7 is a river deer or roebuck (*Chang-tzu*). A work called "Auspicious Pictures," quoted in the encyclopedia *T'ai-p'ing yü-lan* (vol. 4, p. 4021), describes a roebuck that gave birth to 200 offspring, suggesting that the animal is a symbol of fertility. Its body reveals the first timid efforts at shading in Chinese painting.

No. 8 includes images of a winged ram and a wine jar. The word for ram (*yang*) resembles the character for "auspicious" (*hsiang);* since Han times the ram or goat has been regarded as a good omen. Ssŭ-ma Ch'ien's *Historical Memoirs* (*Shih Chi*) contains a passage reading: "The neighbors bring sheep and wine to congratulate two families" [the families of Lo-wan and the Han emperor Kao-tsu], an indication that this animal could be an auspicious symbol (ch. 93, p. 5a). Later, during the period of the Northern and Southern dynasties (fourth-fifth century A.D.), ceramic *Yüeh*-ware wine vessels in the shape of winged rams appeared in tombs found in the Nanking area. The color of the jar in this composition, black on the outside and red inside, suggests lacquerware.

The white hare and two birds shown in no. 9 probably had an auspicious significance also. The Mandarin duck on the left later came to be associated with conjugal fidelity and the *luan* bird on the right is a kind of pheasant or "female phoenix." The heavily damaged plant to the right of this bird is labeled *chih-ts'ao* ("fungus plant"), symbolizing longevity.

Judging from the style of the paintings, all of them would seem to have been painted by the same strong hand. Nos. 7 and 8 are the finest of the series. Even at this early stage we can appreciate the artist's efforts at naturalistic representation, although he had not attained nearly the level of sophistication of the T'ang artist who painted the hound and cheetahs in the tomb of I-te (see no. 134). The colors of these paintings are still bright and brilliant; the mineral yellow and the cinnabar red, as well as the white of the wings, are typical colors in Han wall painting.

The animals and birds were drawn with the same skillful hand as the human figures in the upper register, but the approach is almost completely reversed: outlines are indicated in bold, thick strokes, whereas the fur and wings are formed with delicate brushwork. The heavy outline of the head and back of the roebuck seems to be drawn in one powerful stroke, as if the artist were practicing something resembling "one-stroke painting," the invention of which is attributed to the great fifth-century painter Lu T'an-wei. (It may have existed already in the Han period, however, as a playful drawing engraved in a bronze vessel dated in accordance with 18 B.C. clearly suggests [see *Kaogu,* 1963, no. 2, p. 62, fig. 2].)

7

8

9

10

10
Guards and officials
(north section of upper register of east wall of front chamber)

From titles written next to each figure we know that the man on the left is a functionary directly responsible to the *men-hsia-shih,* or administrative officer, shown on the opposite wall. He is accompanied by eight guards whose duty it is to clear the road for the Master when he travels. The functionary, like his superior on the other wall, is holding a tablet, his badge of office. His body assumes a slightly bent, respectful posture. Possibly because of his lower rank, or perhaps because of his youth—he is the only man without a trace of a beard—he is shown kneeling rather than standing or sitting. According to the chapter on equipages and costumes in the *History of the Later Han Dynasty,* only a Grand Councillor was assigned eight guards, and we may conclude, therefore, that the deceased was a man of that rank. The painter drew them up in two alternating files; six are dressed in a pinkish and yellow uniform, whereas the other two wear black hats and a blue uniform. All are shown as smaller in stature than their immediate superior and, for practical reasons as well as to indicate lower status, their garments are short and have narrow sleeves. At the end of the line is a ceramic basin on a four-legged stand filled with six branches of a certain flowering plant. The inscription identifies the plant as *chieh-huo* (later known as "Buddha's fingernail"). It has been thought since the Han period to have the mysterious power of preventing fire (the literal meaning of *chieh-huo*). Traditionally planted on rooftops or in courtyards (as in this example), the flower blooms in late summer or early fall. This is the earliest known pictorial evidence of a plant commonly described in literary sources. Modern horticulturists have assigned to it the name *Sedum alborosem* or *Sedum erythrostictum miq.*

11
Bookkeeper
12
Master of the Records
(flanking doorway, leading from front chamber into central chamber)

Facing the entrance in a respectful posture as if they were reporting to their deceased master, the two officials are seated on a low couch, an inkstone and water dropper in front of each. Both wear the same headgear and the same black uniform. The bookkeeper has a brush in his right hand and a tablet in his left; the Master of the Records sits with his hands folded in his sleeves. Of all the figures in this tomb these are the only two shown in a seated posture and only they appear with furniture. These considerations, along with their proximity to the remains of the deceased, suggest that they outrank all other officials portrayed here. One of the mortuary gifts found in the tomb is a stone couch (24.5 cm. high) virtually identical with the seats of these two officials.

The straight lines in which the couches are drawn are obviously achieved with the aid of a ruler, an early, if not the earliest example of *chieh-hua* ("ruled and measured" drawing) in Chinese painting. The perspective of the couches follows the traditional Chinese pattern, i.e., making the rear wider than the front. This is the same method as that used for the bed in a scene in Ku K'ai-chih's *Admonitions of the Court Instructress* (see Sickman and Soper, pl. 48a) and completely different from the perspective that was introduced later through Buddhist art.

The three-legged ink-stones in front of the officials constitute the earliest painted evidence for this important writing utensil in China. According to articles by Wang Yeh-ch'iu (*Wen Wu*, 1964, no. 1, pp. 49-52, pl. 1) and Cheng Shao-tsung (*Wen Wu,* 1964, no. 10, pp. 42-43), this is the earliest type of ink-stone used in China. Contrary to what one might expect, the protruding black object is not an ink-cake similar to the types known today, but rather a stone for grinding ink, as can be seen in an actual example of the period. An ink-stone excavated in 1955 from a Han tomb in Hopei Province has a cover shaped to fit over the grinding stone (see *Wen Wu,* 1964, no. 10, p. 42). Three-legged round ceramic ink-slabs of the fourth century A.D., excavated from tombs in the Nanking area, as well as the T'ang examples with many legs, obviously all derive their basic shape from such Han prototypes. That no trace of the ink is to be seen in the wall painting is not surprising. Wang Yeh-ch'iu suggests that the ink was provided in the shape of a pellet and it is quite likely that the pellet was placed in the "pond," the shallow cavity filled with water from the small container beside each of the two officials. The use of this type of ink is documented by the great calligrapher Wang Hsien-chih (A.D. 344-388), who wrote a letter [the original survives in the Shanghai Museum] about the inferior quality of certain ink pellets known as "duck's-head pellets" (*Ya-t'ou-wan*; for the letter see *Shodō Zenshū,* pl. 55). Two inscriptions appear above each official. Chinese scholars have pointed out that the smaller one was a mistake, originally covered by whitewash, that reappeared when the white began to flake. Written in bold script is the proper title for the person portrayed. The painstaking precision with which the artist treated the paraphernalia, as well as the identifying labels, gives a vivid picture of the world in which he and the deceased lived.

The artistic quality of the figure paintings in the Wang-tu tomb would seem to be superior to that of most other paintings. For all their subtlety, the earlier paintings, such as those found in tomb no. 61 at Loyang and the Boston tiles (see p. 10) lack the firmness and confidence of the creations of the Wang-tu painter, a difference especially obvious in the costume, which is strictly linear in the early murals. A trend toward more realistic treatment of garment folds is clearly noticeable in the later style, in which fine lines and bold strokes are used in combination. The earlier tombs have paintings of a distinctive narrative or emblematic character, whereas in Wang-tu an unusually lifelike atmosphere has been achieved, as if the artist had tried to live up to the old Chinese tradition of the *Book of Rites* "to serve the dead as if they were alive." The chamber with the wall paintings, by virtue of its lifelike decoration, was transformed into the court of a high official with factotums ready to serve him in life after death as they had done during his earthly existence.

Excellent photographic color reproductions published in *Murals from the Han to the T'ang Dynasty* afford us an opportunity to establish the accuracy of the copies exhibited here. Although the copy of the *Master of the Records* is basically quite faithful, it does not always convey the extraordinary strength of the original brushwork; the tone of the ink differs quite considerably in some places.

The biography of Ts'ai Yung (A.D. 133-192) in Chang Yen-yüan's *Record of Famous Painters of Successive Dynasties* describes Ts'ai Yung's commission from Emperor Ling-ti (reigned A.D. 168-189) to paint the generals and ministers of state of the marquis of Ch'ih-ch'üan in an official building and his being ordered to compose the accompanying eulogies (see Acker, vol. 2, pp. 11-12). This is yet another piece of literary evidence that in Han times the buildings of the living and the tombs of the dead were decorated with paintings that closely resembled each other in subject matter, as well as in style and technique.

11

12

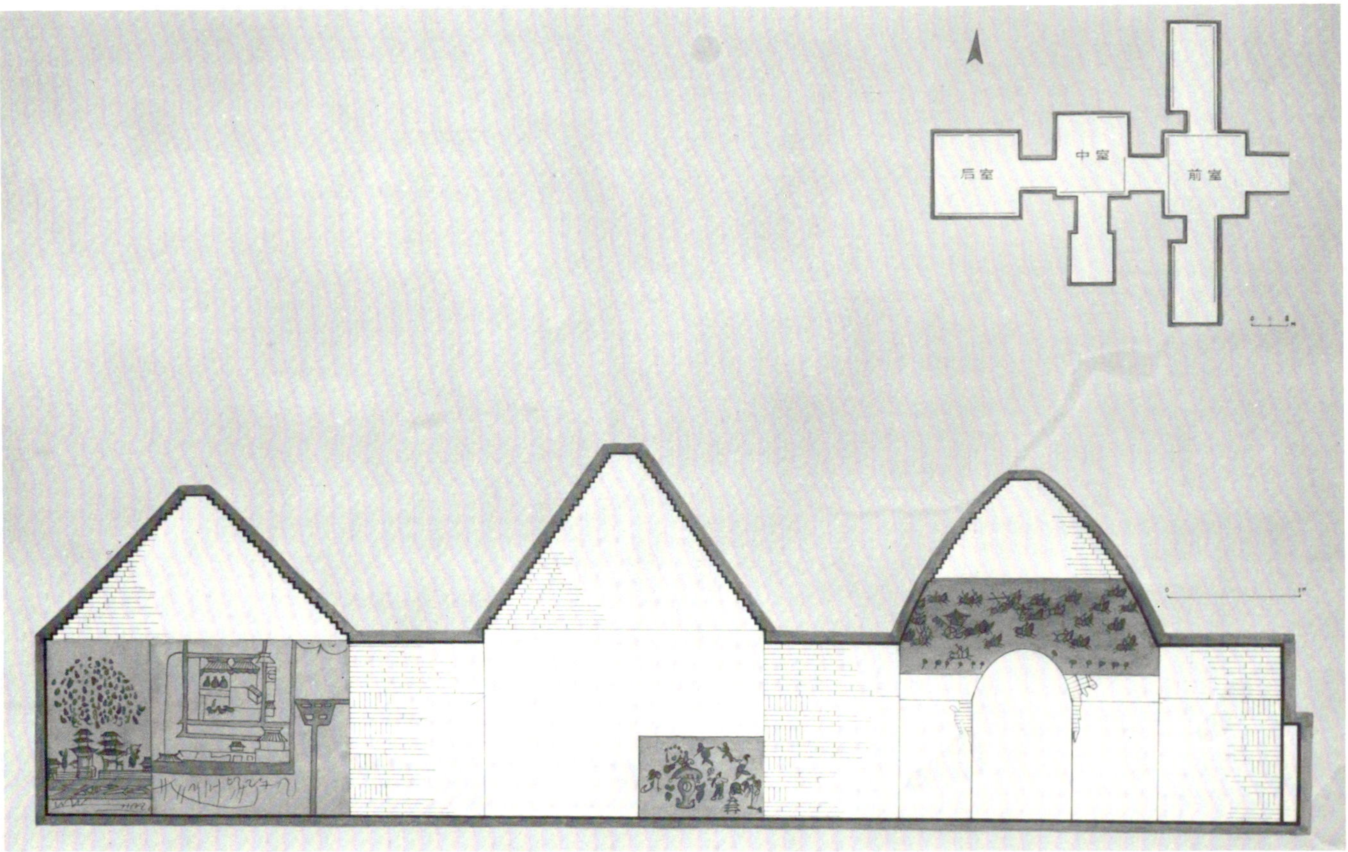

后室

中室

前室

IV

Eastern Han Tomb near Holingol, Inner Mongolia

In the autumn of 1972 a tomb dating from the late Eastern Han period was excavated on the bank of the Red River west of the Hsin-tien-tzu Commune at Holingol, south of Huhehot, the capital of the Inner Mongolian Autonomous Region, and only thirteen miles north of the Shansi border. The tomb is constructed of brick and consists of a passageway and three vaulted chambers. The central chamber has one side chamber, and the front chamber has two side chambers, all connected by vaulted corridors. As the tomb had been robbed, it yielded very few artifacts of importance; its principal interest resides in the more than fifty murals covering the walls of the chambers and corridors as well as the ceilings.

The wall paintings are organized in three layers. The upper register includes stars and supernatural beings; the middle register illustrates activities and key achievements of the occupant of the tomb during his lifetime; and in the lower register are scenes depicting the occupant's servants and followers as well as maps of the towns in which he served as magistrate. There are a large number of inscriptions, more than 225 in all, which are of great historical interest. They are all written in the style of chancery script (*li-shu*) that is typical for the late Eastern Han period. Considerable differences in style and technique between some of the wall paintings indicate that more than one artist worked on them. The archaeologist Huang Sheng-chang reports that another tomb (not as yet published), also decorated with murals, was discovered about 300 feet from this one (*Wen Wu*, 1974, no. 1, p. 44). Its presence could be an indication that several members or generations of one family were buried in a cemetery here. The murals in the tomb at Holingol are of special importance for the vivid visual record they provide of the history and topography of this area during the Eastern Han period. They illustrate life in the far north of China and the contacts of the Han people with local minorities about which we previously had only written information.

13

Cassia tree and twin chüeh towers

(left end of north wall of rear chamber)

The theme of the tree with twin towers is quite common in Han art, occurring in stone reliefs from Shantung in the east to Szechwan in the west of China (see, e.g., Wen Yu, *Ssŭ-ch'uan Han-tai hua-hsiang hsüan-chi*, pl. 82). The tree is usually identified as the solar Tree of Life or *fu-sang* tree, associated with the Taoist search for immortality. In this specific case, however, an accompanying inscription designates the tree as a cassia; therefore, no reference to mythology would seem to be intended here. The legendary archer I, often shown under the *fu-sang* tree while shooting down sun birds, differs from this archer, who seems to aim his arrows into the void, for in this demythologized tree there are no sun birds.

The two *chüeh* towers, an imperial symbol, made their first appearance in the art of the Han period. They continued to be a favorite theme of painters and sculptors who decorated the interiors of tombs as late as the eighth century (see no. 127).

14

City plan of Wu-ch'eng

(right side of north wall of rear chamber)

Like no. 16, this is an early Chinese effort at mapping, in which cartographic projection is combined with buildings shown in elevation and enlivened with human figures and animals. The map includes two sections of a city identified by the inscription as Wu-ch'eng. To the right of it is a stylized column and bracket painted in the same color as the rectangular frame and the city walls. The upper inner part of the city shows gates and houses in elevation as well as figures and horses. The outer part shows only a few carefully labeled buildings, including a South Gate and a County Office Gate. In the lower part of the mural is a roughly drawn sketch, the meaning of which is unclear.

This type of map drawing may have derived from such early prototypes as the maps on silk recently discovered in tomb no. 3 at Ma-wang-tui near Ch'ang-sha, Hunan Province (second century B.C.; see *Wen Wu*, 1976, no. 1, pp. 18-32). According to the Chinese scholars who have made an extensive study of the many historical and topographical questions involved, the county seat of Wu-ch'eng was probably the place where the occupant of this tomb passed the last years of his life. Huang Sheng-chang points out that Wu-ch'eng County was probably less than two miles east of the site of this tomb (*Wen Wu*, 1974, no. 1, p. 42). It lies buried under the present town of Yü-lin-ch'eng, which belonged to Ting-hsiang-chün during the Eastern Han period. In May 1961 a seal impression in clay, once attached to a document, was excavated at nearby Huhehot. It bears the name Ting-hsiang (see *Nei-meng-ku ch'u-t'u wen-wu hsüan-chi*, pl. 85) and would seem to confirm, therefore, this geographic identification.

13

14

15 *See color plate, p. 10.*

Passing through Chü-yung-kuan

(above doorway on east wall of central chamber)

The mural depicts a procession of horsemen and horse-drawn chariots crossing a bridge, with three men floating in a boat underneath. The trapezoidal shape of the bridge with its two sloping ramps echoes the vault of the entrance over which it was painted. (A similar depiction of a bridge across the Wei River appears over the passageway vault on the west wall). Since this copy does not depict the vault it fails to convey the relationship between architecture and decoration in this tomb. Lo Che-wen has suggested that the bridge was given this shape to adapt it to the curve of the vault, and not because actual Han bridges had this structural character (*Wen Wu,* 1974, no. 1, p. 36). However, in view of the fact that the motif of bridge crossings is quite common in Han stone reliefs in Shantung and Kiangsu, and noting that the bridges usually have this same shape, his explanation is not entirely convincing.

The frequency with which crossings appear in Han tombs has led several Western scholars to suppose that the theme should be viewed as an allegory, and that travelers crossing the bridge symbolize the journey of the soul into the afterlife. It is interesting to see that here again, exactly as was the case in the scene of the cassia tree, a demythologized, pragmatic attitude is confirmed by the two inscriptions. The lower one identifies the bridge as that of Chü-yung-kuan, a famous gate station in China's Great Wall; the upper one describes the crossing of the occupant of the tomb en route from Fan-yang (see no. 16) after promotion to the post of colonel-protector of Ning-ch'eng (see nos. 17 and 18). Most Chinese scholars have taken the inscriptions literally, assuming the structure to be a gate, not a bridge. Only Huang Sheng-chang has suggested that the bridge in the mural might be the so-called Blue Dragon Bridge near the southern entrance of the present gate (*Wen Wu,* 1974, no. 1, p. 46).

Although it would seem at first somewhat odd that a gate in the Great Wall would be represented as a bridge, the topographical work *Shui-ching-chu* by Tao-yüan (died A.D. 527) mentions that the gate spanned the river, with access to both land and river routes. Even today, close to the monument, there is a small stream that never dries up completely, although it is shallow most of the time. The crossing of the bridge at Chü-yung-kuan, then, seems to be an actual episode in the life of the occupant of the tomb. (The Chü-yung-kuan, now an architectural monument, is first mentioned in the *History of the Later Han Dynasty* in connection with an event that occurred in A.D. 39.)

16

City plan of Fan-yang

(lower register on left side of doorway to side chamber, south wall of central chamber)

The inscription reads: "yamen of the magistrate of Fan-yang;" on the opposite side is a map of the city of T'u-chün. The occupant of the tomb served as an official in both cities. From the cartographic projection with buildings in elevation it is obvious that maps of this type in printed gazetteers of the Sung and later periods were the product of a tradition that had its origin in the Han.

The city called Fan-yang in Eastern Han times can be identified with the present village of Ch'u-wang (Nei-huang County, Honan Province). It is here that the last emperor of the Eastern Han dynasty abdicated in A.D. 220. The city was afterward renamed Fan-ch'ang, and the fact that the former name is used in the inscription gives us a useful *terminus ad quem* for the murals.

The shape of the city is almost rectangular; crenellated walls divide it into inner and outer segments. The inner city occupies one corner of the outer city, sharing two of its walls, a typical plan for a frontier town of the Eastern Han period that could easily be defended. The visual evidence is at variance with the description of the standard city plan given in the *Chou Li* [*Ritual of Chou*], which states that cities are nine *li* square and that they have three gates on each of the four sides, connecting nine streets running north-south and an equal number running east-west. The Fan-yang plan shows no streets at all. One wall has three gates, two have one, and one has none. According to archaeological reports Western Han cities in the area of Inner Mongolia were usually constructed in the shape of two concentric squares (*Kaogu,* 1961, no. 4, p. 212; and no. 6, p. 340). The fact that Fan-yang and Wu-ch'eng (see no. 14) show a different arrangement suggests that by Eastern Han times a new type of city plan had been adopted.

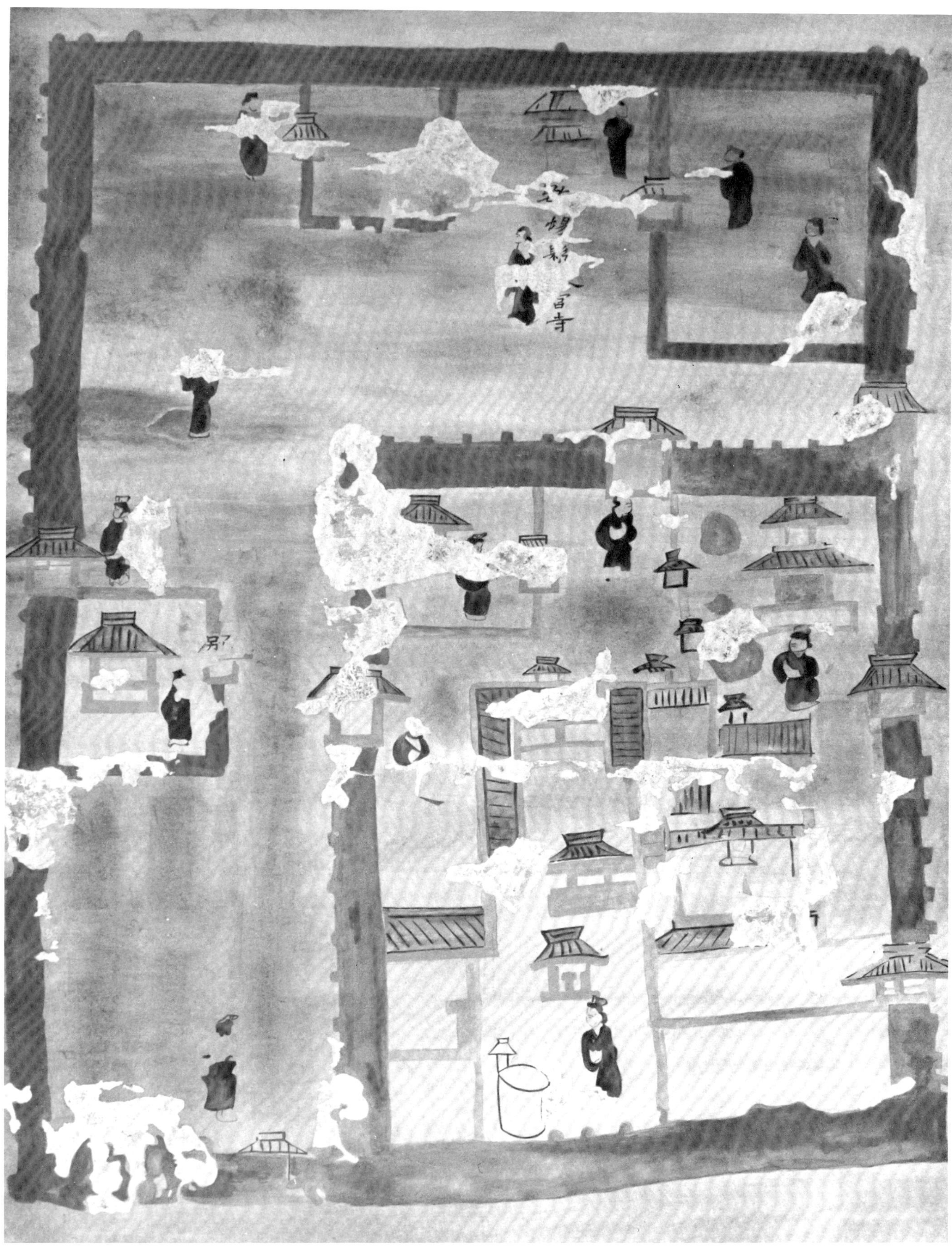

16

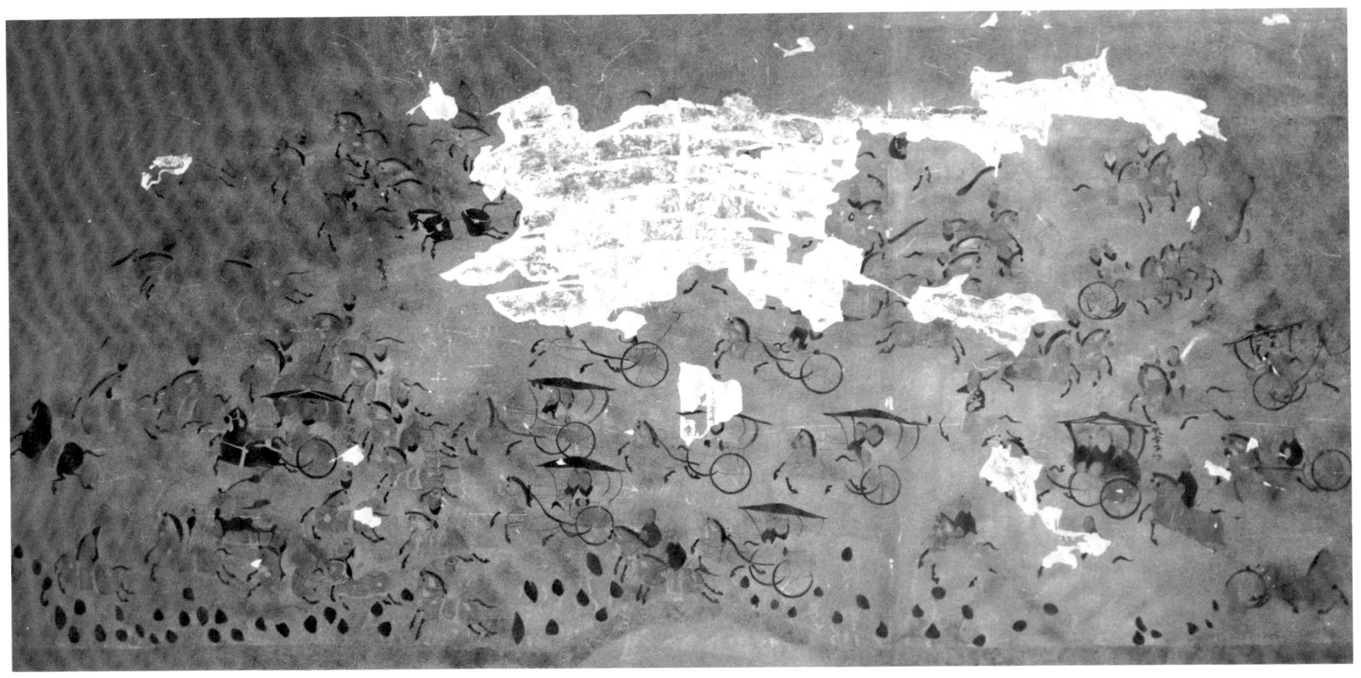

17

19

17-18
Chariot processions

(middle register of west [17] and north [18] walls of front chamber)

All four walls of the chamber are covered with paintings depicting major events in the life of the occupant of the tomb. The scenes are not what we would be inclined to think at first, i.e., pageants of the type usually depicted on the walls of Han tombs, but rather, as indicated by labels, they are a pictorial record—the visual equivalent of a mortuary inscription—of the career of the deceased. Guided by the inscriptions we can follow, from one procession to the next, his gradual rise in the hierarchy from a man selected for official service (*hsiao-lien*) to secretary (*lang*), to magistrate of Hsi-ho, to commander of Shang-chün, to district magistrate of Fan-yang and, finally, to colonel-protector of the Wu-huan tribe.

After each promotion in the career of the tomb's occupant, we see an appropriate increase in the number of escorts in his entourage, from a mere six after his appointment to secretary to more than a hundred after his rise to the office of colonel-protector. Despite the many details of the pictorial *curriculum vitae*, and other information from literary sources, the name of the tomb's occupant is not recorded and the problem of his identity remains unresolved.

The *History of the Later Han Dynasty* mentions that local officials who can read and write reports and who are forty years of age could be promoted to *hsiao-lien,* from which we may conclude that the career of this official started after he had reached that age. Other sources indicate that candidates for promotion to the rank of *lang* should not be older than fifty.

Another passage in the *History of the Later Han Dynasty*, describing the situation shortly after A.D. 140, mentions that the *Shan-yü* (chieftain) of the so-called Southern Hsiung-nu, or Huns, was ordered to move with his tribe to Hsi-ho, where the magistrate was to protect them. Such references give us an idea of the kind of duties that the magistrate of Hsi-ho, who is buried in this tomb, had to perform. Unfortunately, the wall painting that deals in great pictorial detail with frontier life and the affairs of the Han people with the local minorities has not yet been copied, and could not, therefore, be included in this exhibition (*see Wen Wu,* 1974, no. 1, pl. 1).

There are several archaeological finds from this territory that confirm the settling of Hsiung-nu tribes in China's northern region. These include roof tiles with a stamped inscription in Chinese characters reading: *Shan-yü ho-ch'in,* which, roughly translated in modern terminology, means "peaceful coexistence with the chieftain of the Huns through intermarriage" (see *Li I-yu, Nei-meng-ku ch'u-t'u wen-wu hsüan-chi,* pls. 71-72). It is interesting to note that these tiles were excavated near Pao-t'ou, close to a site marked on a 1939 map as the "tomb of Chao-chün." According to tradition, Chao-chün was a beautiful young court attendant from the Han Imperial Palace who was given away by mistake to a chieftain of the Huns. She had refused to bribe the court painter who had, in retaliation, portrayed her unflatteringly. When the emperor had to select the chieftain's bride from a set of portraits, he chose Chao-chün.

Historians have identified the place where the occupant of the tomb served as magistrate of Hsi-ho with the present Li-shih in Shansi Province. He later moved to T'u-chün (the present Shih-lou in the same province) and was transferred from there to Fan-yang (in what is now Nei-huang County, Honan Province). The important position of colonel-protector of the Wu-huan tribe, his last assignment, was established as early as the Western Han dynasty, but historical sources indicate that the seat of this official was moved several times. In A.D. 49, when the chieftain He-tan of the Wu-huan tribe surrendered to the imperial army, the office was moved to Ning-ch'eng, where the occupant of the tomb served. In A.D. 200 it was transferred to Kuang-ning (Liao-ning Province), another indication that the tomb murals are earlier than that date. Moreover, the name Wu-huan (one of the many nomadic tribes that lived in the northern border regions during the Eastern Han period) was changed to Wu-wan after the fall of that dynasty. As the old name is used in the inscription, this is additional proof of the Eastern Han date of this tomb.

Apart from recording an official's rise to a position of power and responsibility, the paintings on these walls illustrate the increased interest of the painters in spatial relationships. The arrangement of figures is much more spontaneous and free than previously, particularly in the skillfully executed U-turn of the chariots in no. 17, which adds great depth and movement to the entire composition.

19
Kitchen scene

(east wall of corridor leading into northern side chamber of front chamber)

In a scene showing food being prepared, a large jar stands on a blazing stove labeled somewhat redundantly with the word "stove," and two men draw water from a well. Above them on a beam hang fish, rabbits, pheasants, and a large cut of meat, all suspended from hooks. This mural can be compared with the barbecue scene in the earlier Lo-yang tomb (no. 2) and with other kitchen scenes in tombs found near Liao-ning (see *Wen Wu*, 1955, no. 5, p. 30, fig. 22; and p. 27, fig. 15).

20
Butchers preparing offerings

In the corridor opposite the preceding kitchen scene, a mural illustrates elaborate preparations for an offering, or, perhaps, for a large funeral party. In the foreground butchers are slaughtering a cow and a ram, beating them with a mallet. (A similar method of slaughtering is illustrated in a painted brick from a tomb at Chia-yü-kuan [no. 79].) In the far background just below the schematic border of curtains, the offering table is shown. Figures move between the tripod vessels and the plates with cups; the whole operation is supervised by two officials seated under the eaves of the two-storied house on the right. One of them is identified by the inscription as an official in charge of offerings.

21
Music, dance, and acrobatics
(lower right corner of north wall of central chamber)

This wall painting presents a marvelous display of various forms of entertainment, carried out for the benefit of a man seated in the upper left corner, accompanied by five women. This is, in all probability, the deceased at the time he was colonel-protector of the Wu-huan tribe. Surrounded by women, food, and wine, he watches the performances: acrobatics, juggling, a whirling dance performed by a couple, a man juggling with swords and one manipulating a wheel, one man standing on his head on top of four tables, another performing the feat of pole balancing. The focal point of the composition is an elaborate drumstand, with a base in the shape of tigers, surmounted by a canopy. Next to the drumstand two drummers vigorously beat a rhythmic cadence to which the artists perform their various acts.

Wu Jung-tseng points out that the headstand on top of the tables and the wheel manipulation are rarely shown in Han art, whereas all the other types of entertainment occur with great frequency (*Wen Wu*, 1974, no. 1, p. 23). There is some literary evidence suggesting that the table trick was imported into China from An-hsi [Parthia]. The first written reference to "manipulating the wheel" occurs in a stele datable to A.D. 220. Murals found in the vicinity of Liao-yang also illustrate the wheel trick (*Wen Wu*, 1955, no. 5, pp. 15-42). It may be significant that the visual evidence for these feats all comes from China's northern border regions, making it likely that these types of performances became popular there during the Eastern Han period and that they spread from there into the central areas of China.

It is interesting to compare the composition of this scene with that of a mural at Mi-hsien (no. 31), where similar performances are depicted. The Holingol picture is typical for the entire tomb in that all activities have been skillfully grouped around a central focal point, presumably in order to create an illusion of depth; in contrast, the Mi-hsien mural has a horizontal arrangement.

22
Drummer, drumstand, and official
(north wall of corridor leading into rear chamber)

Standing next to the drumstand with a base in the shape of crouching tigers and provided with an elaborate canopy is a disproportionately tall figure carrying a sword and a tablet of office. He is described as an official from the palace, while the drum is labeled "big drum." It resembles a large drum in a tomb relief at I-nan (*I-nan*, pl. 88), except that there the base is a simple cruciform stand and the canopy has a bird-shaped finial exactly like one in the *Nymph of the River Lo* in the Freer Gallery. Among the many lacquered drumstands that have been excavated in the southern province of Hunan in recent years, many have both the base in the shape of tigers and a pair of birds as supports for the drum.

23
Farming scene
(northern side chamber of front room on west wall; *Wen Wu*, 1974, no. 1, p. 11, erroneously states south wall)

The wall painting illustrates two agricultural activities, plowing and harvesting, and the way these seasonal tasks are combined visually suggests the continuity of the process. There are two inscriptions: one on the left identifies the conical shapes as piles of harvested grain, and the tripod vessels bear a label reading *hu*, a corn measure equivalent to ten Chinese pecks (*tou*). A farmer loading grain onto a cart is the focal point as well as the logical center of the entire composition. The

20

21

22

23

26

plowmen in this painting, their furrows schematically indicated by broad parallel strokes of the brush, are an interesting contrast to those in T'ang murals (nos. 99-100).

24
Herding cattle

(east wall of southern side chamber of front room opposite no. 26)

Two horse-drawn carts, accompanied by two men on horseback pass a herd of five cows and two heifers. The cows are lined up in a row, all raising right front legs as if on parade.

25
Herding sheep

(east wall of northern side chamber of front room, opposite no. 23)

A herd of sheep accompanied by two shepherds and three sheepdogs pass a frontier fortification, identified as such by an inscription. Two men who are probably grain inspection officials depart from the fortress in a horse-drawn chariot.

26
Horse ranch

(west wall of southern side chamber of front room, just opposite no. 24)

A stylized column and bracket, painted in red, divides the composition, cutting through even the legs of the horses, demonstrating the fact that architectural decoration of tombs is not always as fully integrated into the design of wall paintings as in such murals as no. 28, where the column functions to separate two activities.

A farmhand and seven horses occupy the foreground, with three colts leaping about behind them. In the background are two horse-drawn chariots, each accompanied by a man on horseback. Although the mural is very similar in composition to no. 24, it is far superior in artistic execution.

27
Farming village

(back chamber of tomb, covering entire south wall)

Chinese scholars think that this bucolic scene, located in the mortuary chamber, reflects the peaceful last years of the life of the tomb's occupant. The large number of horses in the center of the composition suggests his interest in horses, and is in keeping with his having spent so much of his life in the frontier region.

In addition to showing a variety of scenery and activities, the mural incorporates two distinct techniques of painting mountains. A wavy line, drawn in one vigorous stroke of the brush, indicates the undulating contours of a mountain range, reduced to its barest essentials. The freedom of the brushstroke is reminiscent of the later *hsieh-i* technique of the literati painters. On the other hand, the mountain in the upper right corner is of a much more complex structure. It is populated by a variety of people, and trees have been planted on it like candles on a birthday cake. This kind of busy activity on the slope of a mountain is not uncommon in Han art; it occurs, for example, on a clay tile from Yang-tzu-shan, Szechwan Province (see *Hsin Chung-kuo k'ao-ku shou-huo*, pl. 84, fig. 1).

A comparison of this mountain scene with one of about a century earlier in a mural at P'ing-lu (no. 4) demonstrates the considerable variety in style of landscape painting during the Han period.

28
Pounding grain in front of a granary

(northern side chamber of front room on north wall)

Architectural decoration of the type simulated here, framing the murals of a tomb, continued into the T'ang period (see nos. 117-19). In addition to the broad bands bordering the composition, a painted column and bracket divides it into two halves. On the left three men stand near five sketchily drawn blocks identified by a label as granaries. On the other side, two men are pounding grain. The entire painting is rather rough and sketchy.

27

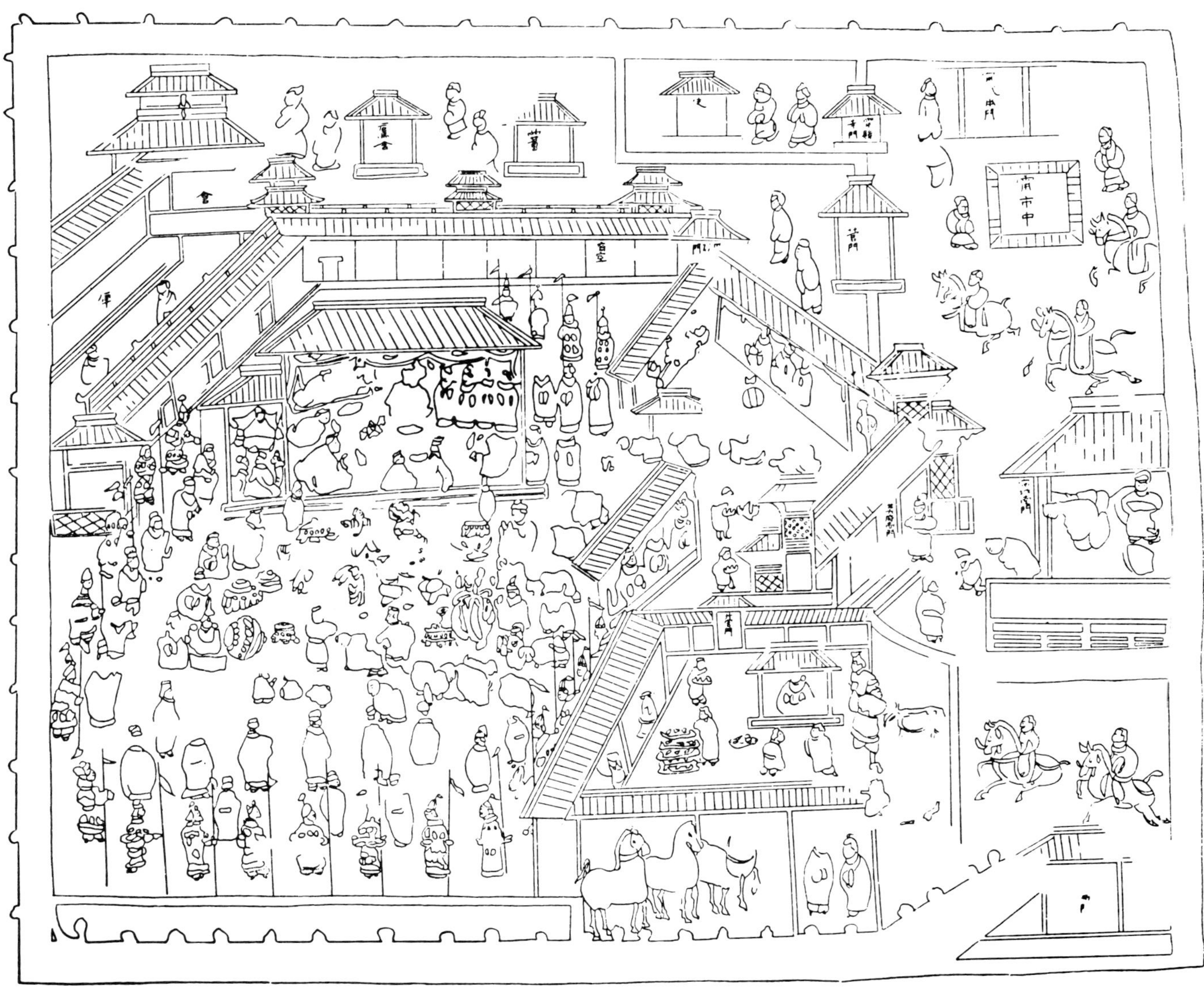

Fig. 2

29

29
Granary

(lower register on north side of west wall of antechamber)

This two-storied building and the figures are all identified by an inscription stating that the granary belongs to the colonel-protector of the Wu-huan tribe, i.e., the deceased. The tall figure in the foreground carrying a sword is probably the official in charge of the granary; immediately behind him are two heaps of grain. The building, with walls of trelliswork for ventilation, is occupied by three persons, two carrying sacks of grain and a third keeping count by means of small sticks. The birds on the roof obviously represent real birds looking for food and not the phoenix-like birds that decorate the pottery models of towers often found in Han tombs.

According to the excavation report a similar granary is shown in the lower register of the south side of the wall, but no reproduction has been published (*Wen Wu*, 1974, no. 1, p. 11). An elaborate picture of the entire office of the colonel-protector located in the lower register of the east wall of the central chamber depicts all important buildings with the exception of the granary (see fig. 2; reproduced from *Wen Wu*, 1974, no. 1, fig. 8).

V

Tomb No. 2 at Ta-hu-t'ing, Mi-hsien County, Honan Province

In 1960 Chinese archaeologists discovered two large tombs, side by side, to the west of the village of Ta-hu-t'ing in Mi-hsien, Honan Province. The larger of the two, designated as no. 1, is distinguished by its fine stone-engraved decoration, whereas no. 2, to be described here, contains a large number of murals. The site had been invaded by grave robbers several times in the past, and no mortuary objects of any consequence were found. The plan of the tomb is rather irregular, consisting of an antechamber leading into a transverse central chamber, with three smaller side chambers on the east and a rear chamber on the north. All are connected by corridors with doors closing off one part from another.

The murals represented here are located in the frieze of the main chamber and on part of its vaulted ceiling. They are painted over a whitewashed brick and stone wall; after a preliminary sketch in ink outline, mineral colors (blue, green, orange, yellow, red, and white) were then applied. The discovery of the tomb was reported in 1960 (*Wen Wu*, 1960, no. 4, pp. 51-52 and 49-50), but it was only in 1972 that it was published in detail (*Wen Wu*, 1972, no. 10, pp. 49-55). This last report attributes the tomb to the late Eastern Han period (end of second century A.D.). The date is based upon the structure and complex layout of the tomb as well as on the subject matter and style of the paintings. Although it is difficult to judge its age without having inspected the original tomb, a comparison with other archaeological finds suggests the possibility that the tomb could date from the period of the Three Kingdoms (A.D. 220-277).

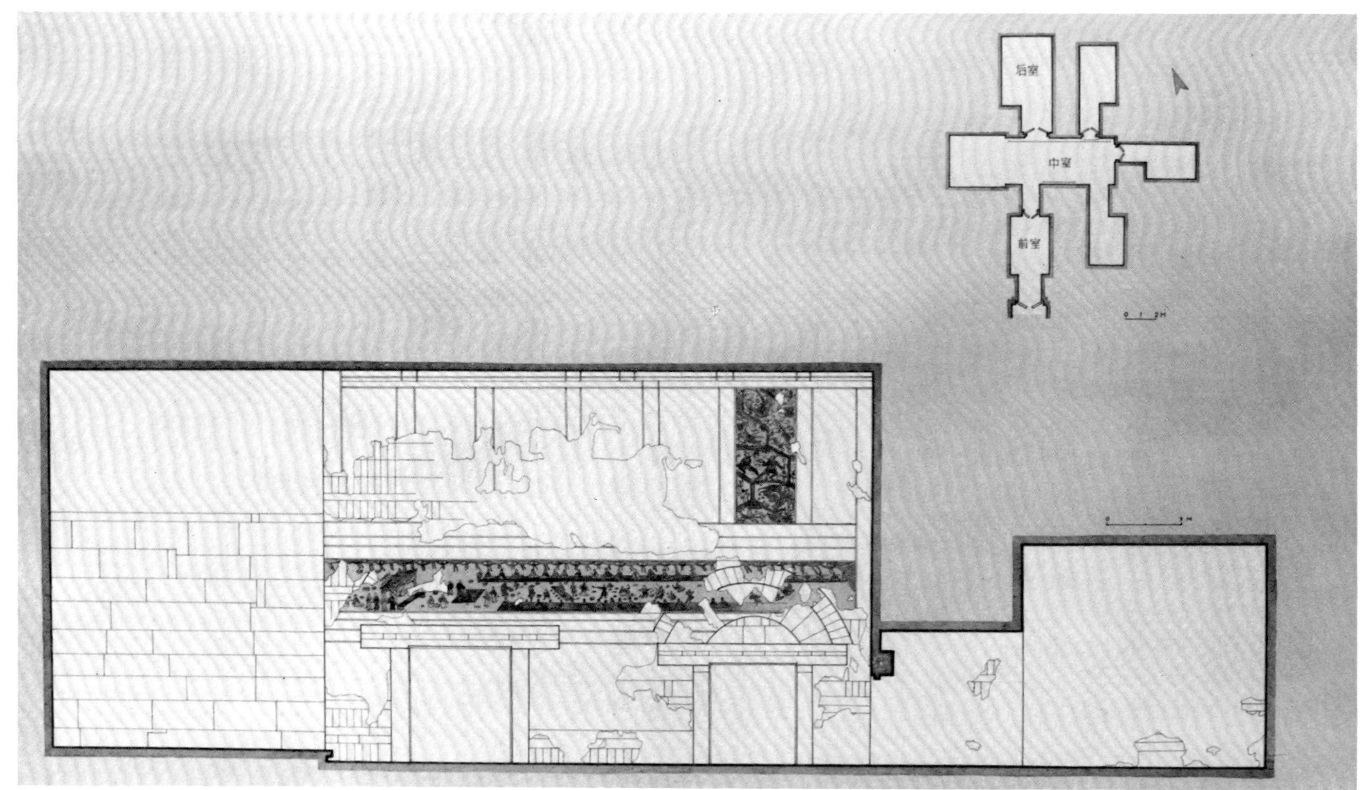

30

31

30
Wrestlers
(east side of vaulted ceiling in central chamber)

The central panel, surrounded by stylized cloud motifs, includes two muscular wrestlers, each clad in a brown loincloth, red shirt, and black shoes. Their hair is knotted on top of their heads, obviously for practical reasons.

This fascinating scene immediately brings to mind two very similar paintings in tombs of kings and noblemen of the Korean kingdom of Koguryŏ, excavated near T'ung-kou, Chi-an County, Liao-ning Province, near the Yalu River (the so-called Tomb of the Dancing Figures and the Tomb of the Wrestlers; see Ikeuchi and Umehara, *T'ung-kou,* pls. 25 and 42-43). Although the Koguryŏ murals date from a slightly later period (fourth or fifth century), they have several features in common with the wrestlers in the Mi-hsien tomb. The hairstyle is practically identical, and the wrestlers strike a characteristic pose strongly reminiscent of postures seen in today's martial arts of China, a discipline that must go back to Chinese antiquity. The earliest pictorial evidence of it is provided by fragments of a painting on silk found in tomb no. 3 at Ma-wang-tui near Ch'ang-sha, Hunan Province (second century B.C.; see *Wen Wu,* 1975, no. 6, pp. 6-13 and 63). This painting shows twenty-eight figures in a variety of martial exercising postures. Some are depicted shoeless and with chest bared like the wrestlers in the Tomb of the Dancing Figures.

An infinite variety of games, pastimes, and sports are shown in Han tombs, but the tomb at Mi-hsien is the only one in which wrestlers appear.

31
Party with musicians and other performers
(upper register of north wall of central chamber)

This oblong frieze measures almost twenty-two feet in length. Above a band of floral scrollwork, and bordered along the top by a typical Han motif of curtains with sashes, an elaborate feast is depicted in vivid detail. On the left is a tent (and not a curtain, as the author of *Murals from the Han to the T'ang Dynasty* maintains) with four flags flying above it. The tent is shaped like a wooden building, and the perspective in which it is shown is identical with that used by the artist of the Wang-tu tomb (see nos. 11 and 12). It recalls the famous bed in the *Admonitions of the Court Instructress* by Ku K'ai-chih (see also p. 31).

Of the figures seated inside the tent only one is clearly visible; perhaps this is the occupant of the tomb. The long table in front of the tent is covered with a variety of sumptuous dishes and what appear to be lacquerware utensils, judging from their black and red color. The guests are seated on mats arranged in a huge U-shape, inside which various performances take place. Among the performers we notice two jugglers, each of whom juggles five balls. Another performer juggles a stick and still another dances around dishes laid out on the floor.

Although the disposition of figures is somewhat reminiscent of the *Paragons of Filial Piety* on the painted basket from a tomb at Lo-lang (National Museum, Pyong-yang), the closest parallels to this tomb are to be found among engraved stones from the tomb at I-nan, Shantung Province. The scroll motif at the bottom of the frieze occurs in several closely related variations in the I-nan tomb (see *I-nan,* pls. 48-49 and p. 55).

32
Horsemen and chariots
(south wall of central chamber)

This frieze, measuring over eight feet in length has been rather severely damaged but, to judge from the remaining details, it would seem to represent the deceased touring in a chariot. The theme is one of the most common in the standard Eastern Han repertoire. A better preserved and much more detailed version can be seen in the tomb at Holingol in the Autonomous Region of Inner Mongolia (see nos. 17 and 18). Later, this subject was replaced by pageants of mounted horsemen, most common during the T'ang dynasty.

VI

Wei-Chin Tombs at Chia-yü-kuan, Kansu Province

A TEAM of the Kansu Provincial Museum and other archaeological organizations carried out three recent excavation campaigns in the Gobi Desert, to the west of the Hsin-ch'eng Commune near Chia-yü-kuan City, Kansu Province. The first, undertaken in April 1972, led to the discovery of four tombs (nos. M1-M4; published in *Wen Wu*, 1972, no. 12, pp. 24-41, pls. 6-8). The second excavation lasted from October 1972 to January 1973 and led to the discovery of three tombs, to which the numbers M5 and M7 were assigned. In September 1973, the final excavation, that of tomb M8, was completed. The last two excavations have not yet been published.

Of the eight tombs that were opened, six contained painted bricks (M1 and M3-M7), altogether more than six hundred in number. The copies shown in this exhibition were made after sixty-four selected pieces from among these finds. The six tombs are all similar in structure, mortuary furniture, and style of decoration. All had vaulted brick chambers and an unusual brick structure simulating a gate tower surmounting the entrance. They had all been previously looted and no longer contained objects of outstanding artistic quality, but in tombs M1 and M2 were pottery jars that are of interest because of their red inscriptions resembling those of jars formerly in the collection of the artist Nakamura Fusetsu (now preserved in the Museum of Calligraphy, Tokyo; see *Shodō Meikan*, p. 11). The inscriptions of the Tokyo jars bear a date corresponding to A.D. 156 of the late Eastern Han period, a date close to that originally assigned to the tombs by the excavators of M1-M4. Later, however, Chang P'eng-ch'uan reexamined the evidence and, after conducting a new analysis of the tomb furniture, concluded that all eight tombs should be attributed to the Wei (A.D. 220-264) and Chin (A.D. 265-419) periods instead (*Wen Wu*, 1974, no. 9, pp. 66-69).

Tombs of similar structure have been found all along the Kansu corridor, the so-called Ho-hsi area. A closer study of them may throw new light on the exact date of the Chia-yü-kuan tombs, as they seem to represent a distinct local style. The earliest of this type to be discovered was excavated by Hsia Nai in June 1944 near Fo-yeh-miao to the southeast of the Tun-huang temple complex (see *Kaogu*, 1955, no. 1, pp. 3-4 and pls. 1-2). This tomb bears a striking resemblance to those at Chia-yü-kuan, sharing the same kind of simulated gate-tower structure, the same kind of painted tiles, and

similar mortuary gifts, including inscribed pottery jars; it was later dismantled and reconstructed at cave no. 143 of the Tun-huang complex. According to an inscription in red on a pottery jar, the occupant of the Fo-yeh-miao tomb was a certain Ti Tsung-ying, whose family belonged to the prominent local gentry. Min Wen-ju has described the tomb of Ti Tsung-ying as the largest in the Tun-huang area, containing no less than 559 painted bricks (*Kuo-hsüeh Quarterly* 7, no. 1, pp. 115-40).

A more recent discovery was a tomb at Hsin-tien-t'ai (not far from Tun-huang) containing an inscription datable to A.D. 369. Although there were no painted bricks in this tomb, its mortuary furniture, again including inscribed jars, is so similar to that of Ti Tsung-ying's tomb that we may date the latter in the same period. The occupant of the Hsin-tien-t'ai tomb was a woman whose maiden name was Ssŭ, another well-known local family (*Kaogu*, 1974, no. 3, pp. 191-99). As tomb M1 at Chia-yü-kuan had an occupant by the name of Tuan Ch'ing, another prominent family in the area, it would seem that tombs of the type described here were all made for members of the ruling class of this strategic locale along the Silk Route.

The sixty-four bricks represented in the exhibition are, with the exception of four, 17 x 36 cm. in size and are decorated with a single painting, most of which are well preserved. Each brick is covered with a thin wash of white plaster and bordered by a brownish red or ochre painted frame. The painting was usually outlined in ink, to which bright colors were added in flat washes without shading. The brushwork is free and spontaneous, sometimes drawn with the sketchiness of simple folk painting. A brush of the type that is likely to have been used to paint these bricks was found in 1972 in a late Eastern Han tomb at Wu-wei, Kansu Province (where the now world-famous flying horse was excavated; see *Wen Wu*, 1972, no. 12, pp. 9-23). Perfectly preserved and labeled "white horse," it is far superior to any of the brushes found in late Chou and early Han tombs.

Viewing the bricks in succession is like looking at leaves in an album. The originals, however, were systematically arranged on the brick walls of the tombs according to subject matter and in a deliberate sequential order. For example, painted bricks in the front chamber of a tomb invariably treated such topics as hunting, farming, cattle-herding, military activities, and other strictly male occupations, whereas those in the rear chamber were concerned with household activities and the silkworm industry, i.e., typical female pursuits. All scenes depicted daily life, often that of the common people; historical narrative dealing with heroes of antiquity and mythology is conspicuously lacking. The bricks can be divided into the following categories according to subject matter: farming (20), household activities (14), cattle-herding (8), hunting (7), silk industry (6), military activities (4), entertainment (3), and camels (2).

It is interesting to note that tombs located along the ancient Silk Route contain many visual references to the silk industry. That is certainly no coincidence, for China's border lands were expected to be economically self-sufficient, and the profitable export of silk to Central Asia was one of the pillars of their economy. The frequency with which military scenes are depicted points to the fact that these areas were settled by farmer-soldiers who tilled the land and protected it against foreign intruders at the same time. This system of military farming (*t'un-tien*) had been established during the Han period, but had fallen into decline during the last century of that dynasty. It received a new impetus during the third and fourth centuries, a development that seems to be reflected in these paintings.

Tomb M1 (nos. 33-39)

33
Inside a frontier stronghold
(west wall of front chamber, north side, fourth register)

34
Plowing
(west wall of front chamber, north side, fourth register)

35
Shepherd with goats and cows
(west wall of front chamber, north side, third register)

36
Falconers hunting
(west wall of front chamber, north side, second register)

37
Cattle drinking at a well
(north wall of front chamber, west side, fourth register)

38
Women carrying water jar to a well
(east wall of front chamber, south side, fifth register)

39
Mounted hunters
(north wall of front chamber, west side, second register)

Of the eight tombs excavated at Chia-yü-kuan the one to which the number M1 was assigned is probably of a slightly earlier date than the others. This may explain why the composition of the paintings sometimes has a somewhat archaic appearance, especially in nos. 33-35. No. 33 shows an aerial view of a frontier stronghold, in which a house, trees, and animals are similar to those on maps in the Holingol tomb (see nos. 14 and 16). The composition in two registers, as seen also in no. 34, is quite close to a farming scene at Holingol (no. 23). It would appear that all of these paintings carry on a pictorial tradition of the late Eastern Han period.

No. 36 is an early example of the mannerism later described by art critics as *chien-shang-fei-wen* ("flying lines over the shoulder"); it appears at about the same time in the mid-fourth-century tomb murals of a king of the Korean kingdom of Koguryŏ (see Fontein and Wu, *Unearthing China's Past*, pp. 229-31). This typical treatment of garment folds around the neck and on the shoulders must have had its origin in Han painting, where we see it in its most rudimentary form in the murals of the Wang-tu tomb. The hunters in no. 39 are obviously of the same ethnic type as the falconers.

A typical difference between the style of the Chia-yü-kuan paintings and the *Admonitions* in the British Museum (see p. 12) or the lacquer screen in the tomb of Ssŭ-ma Chin-lung (see p. 20) is the total absence of floating and flying scarves. The variation is probably due only to the difference in class of the persons depicted: common people portrayed in the bricks from Chia-yü-kuan would have had no use for elegant scarves or sashes that would have interfered with their manual labor.

33

34

35

36

37

39

Tomb M3 (nos. 40-53; 95-96)

40
Plowing scene
(east wall of front chamber, south end, third register)

41
Farming couple winnowing grain
(east wall of front chamber, north end, third register)

42
Leveling the soil with a roller
(south wall of front chamber, east end, third register)

43
Boy and buffalo
(west wall of front chamber, north end, fifth register)

44
Preparing noodles
(south wall of front chamber, west end, third register)

45
Two musicians
(center of west wall of front chamber, fifth register)

46
Mounted hunter
(east wall of front chamber, north side, second register)

47
Farmer harrowing
(south wall of front chamber, east side, fourth register)

48
Ox and cart
(center of west wall, central chamber, fourth register)

49
Butcher slaughtering a goat
(center of west wall, central chamber, fifth register)

50
Rooster and hens
(west wall of front chamber, north side, second register)

51
Three horses
(west wall of front chamber, north side, second register)

52
Straining of vinegar
(east wall of front chamber, north end, fourth register)

53
Two musicians
(west wall of front chamber, south end, sixth register)

95
Soldier-farmers
(south wall of front chamber, west end, first register)

96
Soldiers' encampment
(south wall of front chamber, east end, first register)

All of the paintings in this tomb have been executed rather sketchily; nevertheless, their simple spontaneity has a rustic charm, and several scenes illustrate life along China's frontiers in a rather interesting manner.

Nos. 95 and 96 are among the few tiles of a larger than standard size (approximately 66 x 102 cm.). They were placed side by side over a gateway in the tomb, and they are of considerable interest as documents of the lifestyle of the military in border regions. No. 96 shows the military commander seated in a tent that resembles the later Mongolian *yurt*. Although the curtains indicate a certain level of comfort, the tent is entirely without furniture. In *Lady Wên-chi's Return to the Han Court*, the famous Northern Sung painting in the Museum of Fine Arts, presumably depicting frontier life of approximately the same era, the artist has furnished the tents with low tables and stands (see Fontein and Wu, *Unearthing China's Past*, pp. 221-25).

44

45

49

51

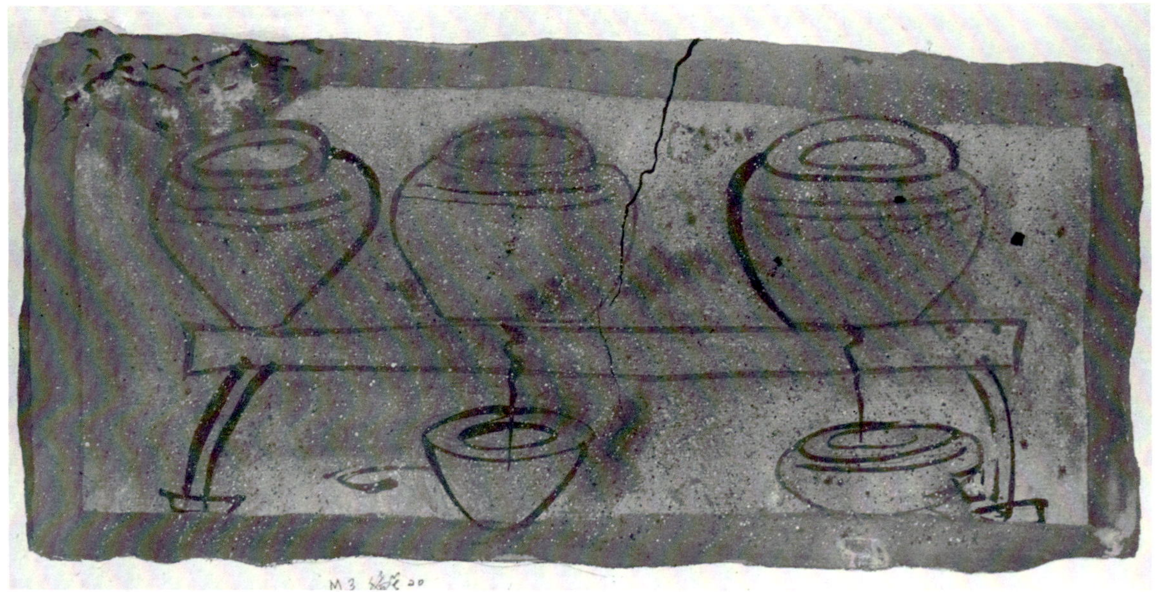

52

53

95

96

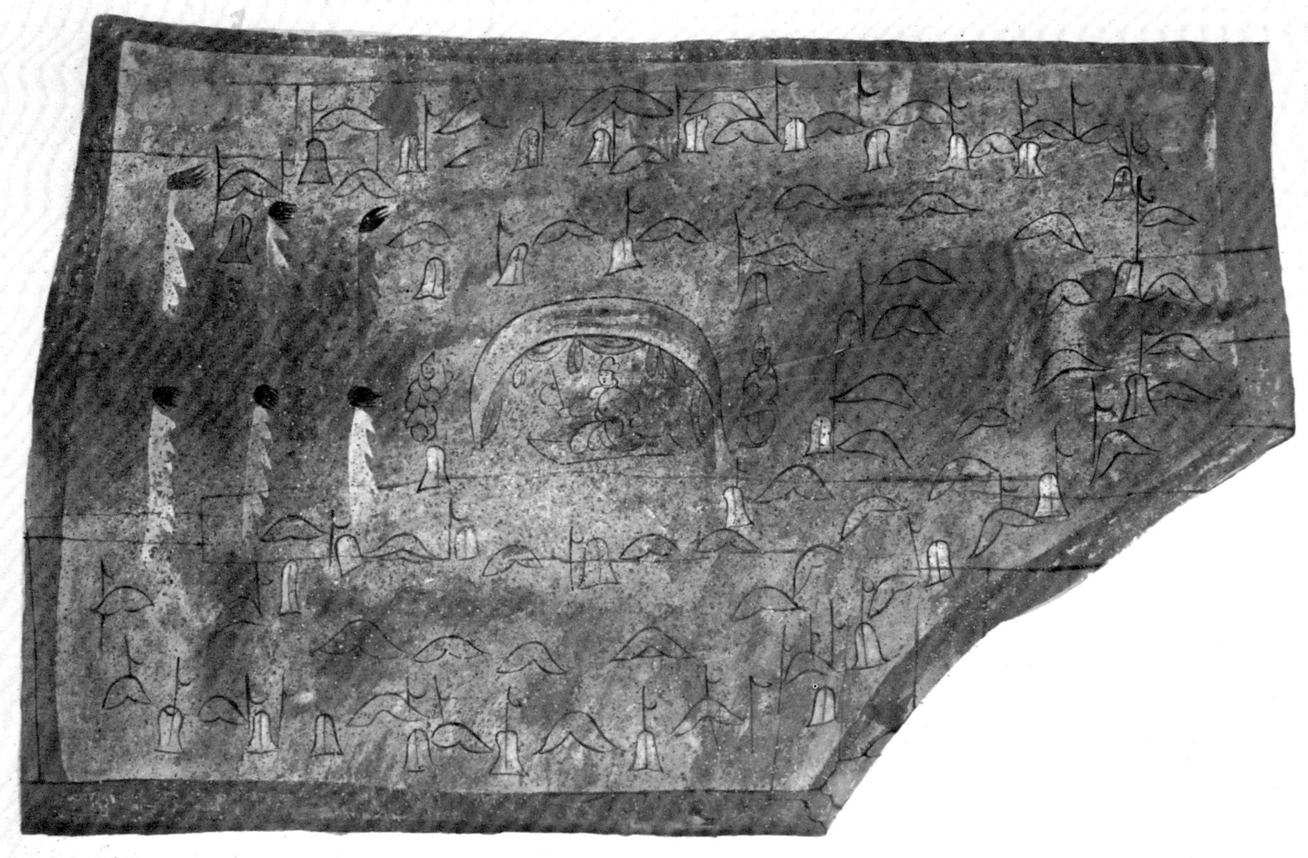

56

Tomb M4 (nos. 54-59; 94)

54
Two farmers: one hoeing, one sowing
(east wall of front chamber, north end, second register)

55
Farmer and dog
(east wall of front chamber, north end, second register)

56
Two farmers and a goat
(east wall of front chamber, south end, first register)

57
Serving food
(west wall of front chamber, south end, first register)

58
Family with covered cart
(west wall of front chamber, north end, second register)

59
Two musicians
(west wall of front chamber, north end, second register)

94
Mounted hunter chasing deer
(north wall, west side, and west wall, north side, of front chamber, second register)

In nos. 56 and 57 two people carry a similar type of jar. The one in no. 56 would seem to have three legs, but that of no. 57 obviously has a base consisting of two ridges. Exactly the same type of jar was found in the tomb of the famous general Chou Ch'u (A.D. 242-297) at I-hsing, Kiangsu Province (see fig. 3; reproduced from *Kaogu Xuebao*, 1957, no. 4, pl. 3c) and might be of help in the dating of the Chia-yü-kuan tombs.

In nos. 56 and 58 two young women are shown with two tufts of hair tied up on top of their heads. The same type of hairstyle can be seen in the handscroll *Scholars of the Northern Ch'i Dynasty Collating the Classics* (Museum of Fine Arts, Boston).

No. 94 is of a different size and shape, measuring 17 x 80 cm.

Fig. 3

57

58

Tomb M5 (nos. 60-76; 93)

60
Plowing
(east wall of front chamber, south side, third register)

61
Leveling the ground with a roller
(east wall of front chamber, south side, fourth register)

62
Harrowing
(east wall of front chamber, south side, third register)

63
Threshing
(east wall of front chamber, south side, fifth register)

64
Winnowing
(east wall of front chamber, south side, third register)

65
Herdsman with six horses
(east wall of front chamber, north side, second register)

66
Farmer with seven cows
(east wall of front chamber, north side, second register)

67
Gathering mulberry leaves
(north wall of front chamber, east side, second register)

68
Guarding mulberry trees
(south wall of front chamber, west side, second register)

69
Mounted hunter chasing a rabbit
(north wall of front chamber, east side, first register)

70
Two camels
(west wall of front chamber, south side, fifth register)

71
Mounted courier
(north wall of front chamber, east side, fourth register)

72
Women plucking chickens
(west wall of front chamber, north side, third register)

73
Butcher slaughtering a pig
(north wall of front chamber, west side, fourth register)

74
Farmer and pigsty
(west wall of front chamber, south side, second register)

75
Plowing
(east wall of front chamber, south side, third register)

76
Gathering mulberry leaves
(center of east wall, front chamber, second register)

93
Parading cavalry
(east wall of front chamber, north side, fifth register)

Although some of the painted bricks found in this tomb were briefly referred to in the 1972 excavation report, these pieces have never been fully published.

The garden of mulberry trees in no. 68 is surrounded by a wall and guarded by a young man with a whip for chasing away birds, one of which flies over the trees. The mulberry is the same roughly stylized tree of no. 67, where a young peasant is seen gathering leaves in a basket. The same type occurs in nos. 69, 70, 74, and 76.

Of particular interest are the paintings illustrating the preparation of food (nos. 72 and 73) and the pigsty of no. 74. One sees through the crenellated walls of the pigsty the vague shape of the pig inside, a simple but effective device to show not what can actually be seen but what is known to be there.

Brick no. 93, like 94 and 96, is of a larger size (46 x 132 cm.). In many ways it is reminiscent of the Han style as recorded in the murals of Holingol, but the soldiers bringing up the rear, wearing armor and helmets, are a novelty not seen there.

60

61

62

63

64

65

66

67

68

69

70

71

72

73

76

93

Fig. 4

Tomb M6 (77-84)

(For an interior view see fig. 4; reproduced from *Murals from the Han to the T'ang Dynasty*, pl. 42.)

77
Plowing
(south wall of front chamber, east side, fifth register)

78
Harrowing
(south wall of front chamber, east side, fifth register)

79
Butcher slaughtering an ox with a mallet
(east wall of front chamber, north side, second register)

80 *See color plate, p. 2.*
Man leading a camel
(north wall of front chamber, west side, second register)

81
Gathering mulberry leaves
(center of east wall, front chamber, second register)

82
Man leading an ox cart
(south wall of front chamber, west side, third register)

83
Man preparing shashlik
(east wall of central chamber, south side, third register)

84
Gathering mulberry leaves
(south wall of front chamber, east side, second register)

Painting no. 83 stands out among the contents of this tomb for its exceptional artistic quality. The picture is unusual not only because it illustrates an exotic type of food, but also for the fact that the person preparing the shashlik seems to be of a different social status than the other figures here. He sits at ease, the curving lines of his garments draped about him so lightly that it looks almost as if he were floating in air. This elegant painting bears surprising resemblance, both in spirit and in execution, to the well-known style of Ku K'ai-chih, the late fourth-century figure painter from the eastern coast of China (see, for example, the British Museum's *Admonitions of the Court Instructress* [fig. 5]; reproduced from Kohara, *Kokka*). Markedly different from a rather formal, controlled mainstream tradition that proceeded from the Han period in the late second century (see nos. 10-12) to the high T'ang (see, for example, no. 141), the Chia-yü-kuan–Ku K'ai-chih style, with its elegant curving forms, seems, nevertheless, to have strong affinities with some examples of Han painting. The same airy, expressive touch is visible in the figure painting on the lintel of the Lo-yang tomb (see no. 2), as well as in the figures engraved in stone from the tomb at I-nan (see fig. 6; reproduced from *I-nan*, pls. 55-60; for further discussion of the issue, see Lawton, *Chinese Figure Painting*, pp. 3-4).

77

78

79

81

82

83

84

Fig. 5

Fig. 6

Tomb M7 (nos. 85-92)

85
Gathering mulberry leaves
(east wall of front chamber, south side, second register)

86
Mounted hunter chasing a wild goat
(east wall of front chamber, south side, third register)

87
Butcher slaughtering a deer
(west wall of central chamber, south side, third register)

88
Kitchen scene
(north wall of central chamber, east side, third register)

89 *See color plate, p. 2.*
Hound chasing a fox
(north wall of central chamber, east side, third register)

90
Kitchen scene
(south wall of central chamber, east side, third register)

91
Kitchen scene
(west wall of central chamber, south side, fourth register)

92
Horse-drawn cart
(center of west wall of front chamber, third register)

Although there are several scenes depicting a butcher at work, none matches the vivid portrayal of no. 87. The same subject shown in no. 49 is far less effective. Nos. 86 and 89 also convey a sense of rapid movement and suspense that is lacking in most of the other hunting scenes. It is obvious that painters of different artistic ability were commissioned to decorate these tombs. Another difference, also of a personal character, can be observed in the unique ways in which artists stylized mulberry trees (e.g., nos. 84 and 85).

86

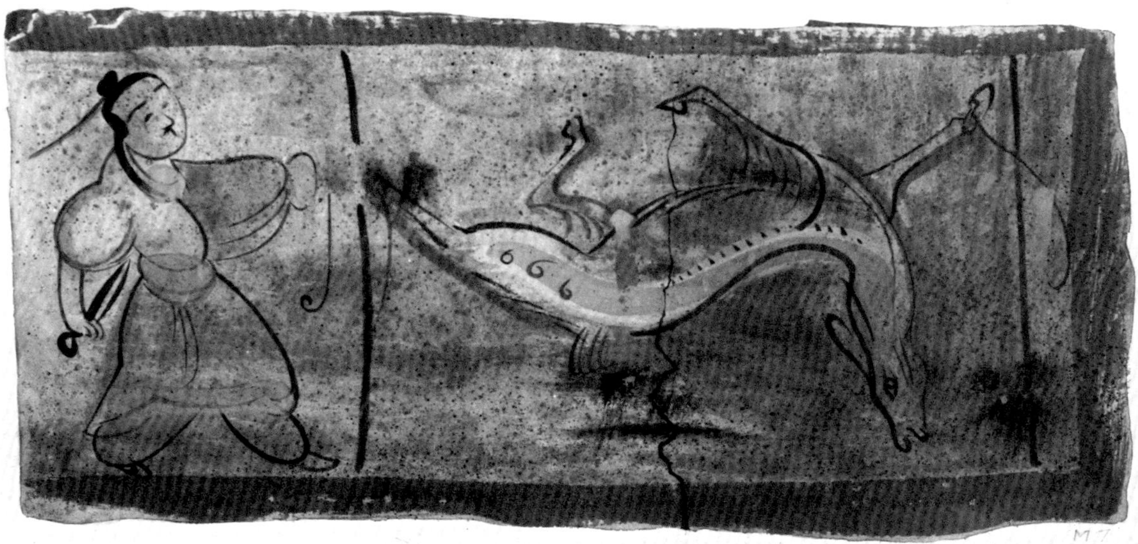

87

VII

T'ang Tomb of Li Shou, Prince Huai-an

Li Shou, Prince Huai-an, was the grandson of T'ang T'ai-tsu and a cousin of the founder of the T'ang dynasty, Li Yüan (who reigned as Emperor Kao-tsu from A.D. 618 to 626). According to the mortuary inscription unearthed from his tomb, Li Shou died during the twelfth moon of the fourth year of the Chen-kuan era, corresponding to the period between January 8 and February 7, A.D. 631. He was buried a year later, on January 8, A.D. 632 (and not 630, as the reports indicate), at a site in what is now the Ling-ch'ien Commune, San-yüan County, Shensi Province. The tomb was discovered by farmers in 1972, when its ceiling caved in after a rainstorm, and it was excavated by a team of archaeologists from the Shensi Provincial Museum between March and August of 1973.

In front of the tumulus, about twenty-five feet high, stand two stone columns and three pairs of stone statues representing officials, tigers, and rams. The tomb itself consists of a sloping outer passageway with four compartments, five vertical air shafts, two small niches, an inner passageway, and a mortuary chamber. The entire structure is over 133 feet long and 7 feet wide.

Although the tomb had been robbed twice in the past, more than 300 mortuary objects were found intact. The most interesting features of the tomb are the paintings covering most of the interior walls. Their subject matter includes hunting, farming, and other occupational pursuits; music and dancing; and pageantry of soldiers. The paintings were made on whitewashed walls sized with glue. With the exception of those on the walls of the inner passageway, all were painted directly onto the wall without preliminary charcoal drawings. As the layer of whitewash was very thin and flaked easily, most are not well preserved. Several sections have been lost entirely, and the copies and photographs shown here represent only a small part of the original tomb decoration.

The walls of the sloping outer passageway have been divided by a broad, straight band of cinnabar red into an upper and a lower register. This method does not seem to have been used in other T'ang tombs, but it is reminiscent of several sixth-century caves in the Buddhist cave-temple complex of Tun-huang in Kansu Province. As for the drawing technique, there is liberal use of the so-called iron-wire lines, i.e., lines of varying thickness, freely drawn and displaying great strength and firmness. It recalls Chang Yen-yüan's description of the brushwork of the great T'ang painter Wu Tao-tzu (see p. 17).

The main colors used are cinnabar red (*chu-sha*), umber, (*che-shih*), rattan yellow (*t'eng-huang*), mineral blue (*shih-ch'ing*), and mineral green (*shih-lu*). They have been applied both in flat washes covering large sections of the painting and as shading on faces and costumes.

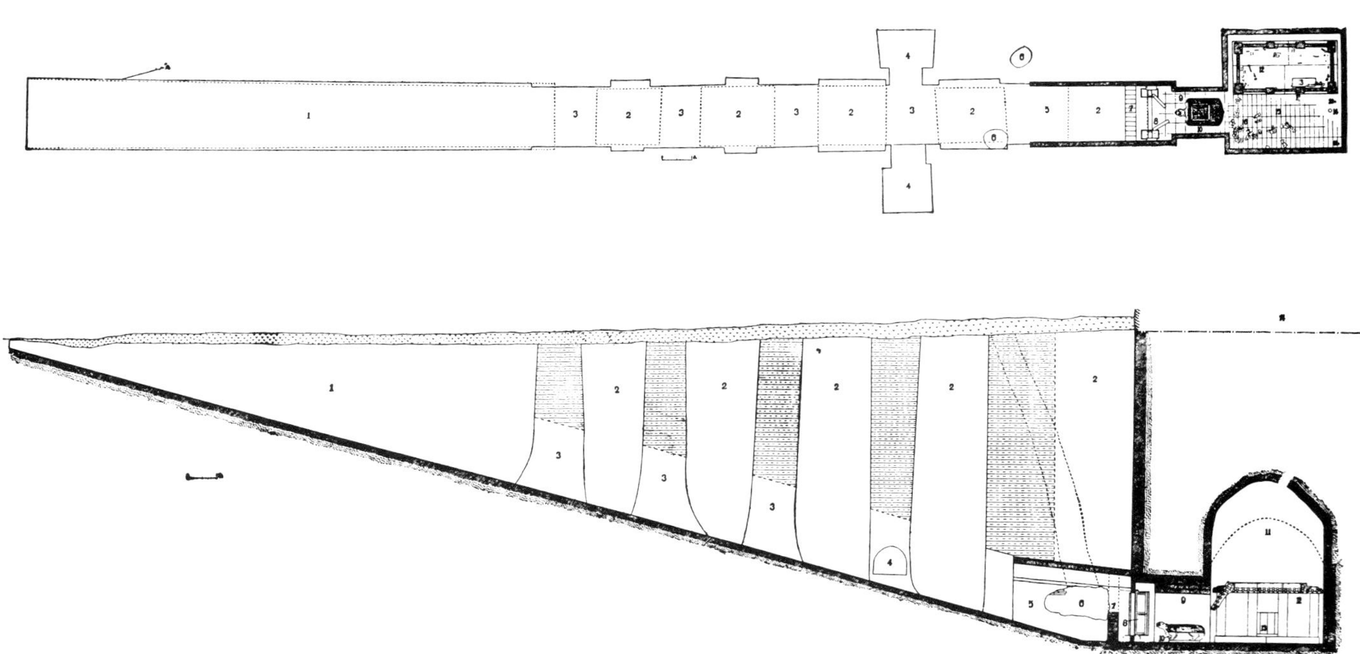

93-96
See pp. 60, 64, and 66.

97
Hunting scene
(upper register of east wall of sloping outer passageway)

This scene occupies about one third of the entire composition (for a drawing of the complete composition see *Wen Wu,* 1974, no. 9, p. 80 [fig. 16]). It shows five hunters on horseback chasing wild boar and deer toward a valley. On the extreme left the eaves of the roof of a tower are just visible. The season appears to be late autumn; small trees scattered throughout the composition are all bare. Hills and rocks are simply outlined without texture strokes. Occasionally, as, for example, on a rock in the background, there is light shading comparable to that on some of the costumes. Perhaps this is a first effort to render the texture of rocks, an indication that this wall painting is a transitional link between the technique of the Six Dynasties period and that of the high T'ang.

The hunters can be compared with those in Northern Wei wall paintings at Tun-huang or a Western Wei hunting scene datable to A.D. 538 (see *Wall Paintings of Tun-huang,* pls. 28, 48, and 62). During the sixth and early seventh century the spatial arrangement of different components and of proportions of human figures, mountains, trees, and buildings faithfully reflects a phenomenon already observed by Chang Yen-yüan: "Sometimes the waters have no room to float [a ship]; sometimes people are [drawn] larger than the mountains" (Acker, vol. 1, p. 154). The hunting scene in Li Shou's tomb is clearly at the watershed of change from an archaic to a more developed concept of landscape painting observable in later T'ang tombs. The horses, of a sturdy breed quite distinct from the stylized horses of previous periods, predict the fashion in horses of the high T'ang, as, for example, in the early eighth-century tombs of Li Hsien and Li Chung-jun (see pp. 90-120).

98
Courtyard scene with musicians and dancing girls
(eastern end of north wall of mortuary chamber, according to excavation report [*Wen Wu,* 1974, no. 9, p. 83]; two other sources place it in third compartment of passageway)

This copy represents only the lower left corner, about one third, of the entire composition. Four servants guarding a gate appear in pairs next to halberd stands. A dancing girl waits in the doorway, which is drawn in the type of perspective often seen in Buddhist painting. Inside the enclosure, painted in typical *chieh-hua* ("ruled and measured") fashion, are five seated female musicians ready to perform on various musical instruments: the five-stringed *p'i-p'a,* the four-stringed *p'i-p'a,* the mouth organ *(sheng),* the harp, and the lute *(cheng).* Behind them stand four maids holding a variety of utensils. Of another dancing girl only the sleeve is visible.

According to the famous T'ang poet Po Chü-i, "seated musicians" were of the highest rank and "standing musicians" were subordinate (Po-Chü-i, ch. 3/3b-4a). The fact that "seated musicians" are depicted in Li Shou's tomb is in keeping with the high rank and status of the deceased. (Both types appear also in tomb figurines of the T'ang dynasty.)

The striped costumes worn by the musicians and the maids, as well as their flat hairdos, are still reminiscent of Sui fashion, but the manservants at the gate, bent slightly forward—as was required of servants—show the respectful attitude that was commonly seen throughout the T'ang period.

97

98

99-100
Plowing and seeding

(upper register of north wall, third compartment of outer passageway, according to *Kita Kyūshū* and *Han-T'ang pi hua;* according to *Wen Wu,* 1974, no. 9, p. 73, they were actually found in the third air shaft)

These two paintings were originally part of a considerably larger wall painting (for what remains of the entire composition, see *Wen Wu,* 1974, no. 9, p. 74, fig. 5). They are the earliest known T'ang portrayals of plowing and seeding, reflecting the rural way of life in China during the seventh century. However, the figures are clad not in the customary farmers' attire but in military dress. In view of Li Shou's military career, we may see them as "soldier-farmers," institutionalized already during the Han dynasty as a means of settling newly occupied areas (see also no. 95).

In no. 99 the plow with a curved shaft makes its first appearance. It is almost identical with a plow excavated at the San-men Gorge, Honan Province (see *Kaogu,* 1964, no. 7, p. 358), and is a technical improvement over the older types shown in wall paintings from P'ing-lu, Shansi Province (no. 5) and from Chia-yü-kuan, Kansu Province (nos. 34, 40, 60, 75, and 77).

The seeding tableau shows a soldier-farmer driving an ox-drawn, two-legged seeder through a freshly plowed field, indicated by the straight parallel lines. According to literary as well as archaeological evidence, the seeder was used as early as the Han dynasty (see *Wen Wu,* 1966, no. 1, p. 23, fig. 44). The seeder in the wall painting at P'ing-lu (no. 4) does not carry a seed container, as appears in later examples, and the *Book of Plows and Plowshares (Lei-ssŭ-ching)* by Lu Kuei-meng (ninth century, A.D.) does not even mention such a container. The illustration in Li Shou's tomb is, therefore, of considerable documentary value.

101-102
Cattle and cart

(location identical with that of nos. 99 and 100)

One of these wall paintings shows cattle leaving a barn, the other an ox-drawn cart. The cattle in no. 101 are drawn with skill, especially in the varying positions of the heads and the animated motion of the legs. Compared to earlier renderings of a similar theme, such as the wall painting at Holingol, dating from the second half of the second century A.D. (see no. 24) and those of Chia-yü-kuan of the late third to fourth century A.D. (see nos. 35 and 66), the paintings in Li Shou's tomb show a distinct advance in representational technique.

The gate of the barn is drawn in the "iron-wire" style, with the "ruled and measured" technique typical of the Sui style. (For a type of line drawing that replaces the earlier technique, see no. 115.) No. 102 shows a man leading an ox and a woman seated in a cart made of planks.

103
Courtyard

(floor of third air shaft, according to excavation report; *Kita Kyūshū* assigns it to north wall, third compartment of passageway)

Although only fragmentarily preserved, this large (125 x 89 cm.) wall painting is of considerable interest, being a rare depiction of family life in the early T'ang period. It shows a compound consisting of a main hall with two lateral buildings, together enclosing a courtyard. In it are seven women busy at household tasks: grinding grain, carrying water jars, tending an infant, feeding chicken, and bringing in plates and cups, obviously in preparation for a meal. The composition appears to be well organized and full of vitality. Even such small details as bowls and jars are depicted with faithful accuracy, as is proved by comparison with actual excavated examples of the same type. Here again the "ruled and measured" architectural details are all drawn in the thin lines of the Sui style, but the more naturalistic proportions seem to demonstrate advancements of the early T'ang.

99

100

101

102

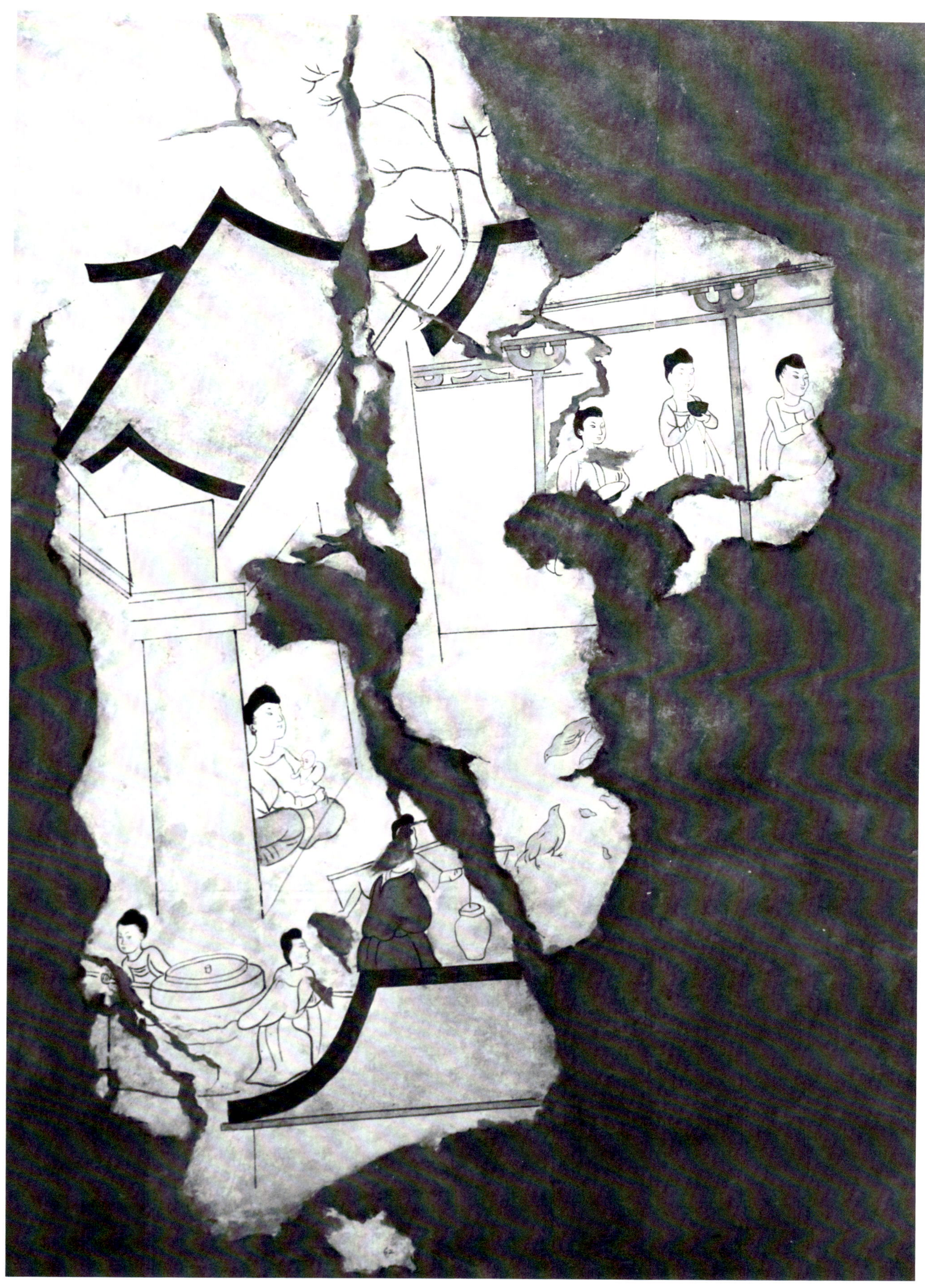

103

104-105
Mounted guards
(east wall of corridor)

Comparison with photographs of the original indicates that less space surrounds the figures there than in the copies. Each group consists of eight riders and their horses, five in front, three in the rear. Like the cattle in no. 101, the horses are all shown in slightly different poses, the second from the right in no. 104 depicted *en face*. The chest and hindquarters are indicated in sweeping curves of "iron-wire" lines, the prototype for the technique of such eighth-century masters as Han Kan and Ts'ao Pa. The riders display considerable variety in pose and facial expression; they are shown straight on and in three-quarter profile. Many tomb figurines are represented frowning, in mourning for their masters, and this is suggested by the solemn expressions here.

Pageants of mounted honor guards made their first appearance in the decoration of Han tombs, but at that time the horse-drawn chariot was the principal subject, whereas horses and riders occupied a secondary position. During the Northern and Southern dynasties new elements such as ox-drawn carts were added to the pageants and it was only at the beginning of the T'ang dynasty that horse guards gained primacy. Quite possibly this change is attributable to the influence of lifestyles of Turkish and Uighur tribes. It could also reflect a penchant for exoticism inherited from the preceding Northern dynasty, a characteristic visible not only in material culture, but also in the fine arts.

106
Saddled horse and servants
(lower register of west wall of passageway, close to antechamber)

This rare masterpiece of early T'ang horse painting is the last section of the continuous sequence in which the pageant (shown also in nos. 104, 105, and 107) comes to its logical conclusion.

Two fans held up behind the horse indicate the elevated status of the deceased. According to Hsü Chien's *Ch'u-hsüeh-chi*, the privilege of having such fans was restricted to princely rank (see ch. 25). The fans and the canopy can be compared with those in a painting attributed to Yen Li-pen in the Palace Museum, Peking. It illustrates a story of a Tibetan king who came to the T'ang court to marry Princess Wen-ch'eng (see *T'ang Yen Li-pen pu-nien t'u*, Peking: Wen Wu Press, 1959, pl. 1). Here it is none other than the Emperor T'ai-tsung who is shown with these accoutrements of imperial dignity.

The horse in this composition is disproportionately large compared with the attendants. The solemn static character of the animal (rendered as a line drawing in contrast to a carefully modeled imperial horse attributed to Han Kan; fig. 7; reproduced from Sickman and Soper, pl. 71) is probably associated with its mortuary function. The *Li-tai ming-hua chi*, describing early T'ang horse painting, says: "They preferred an appearance of prancing and rarely showed them in peaceful and leisurely guise" (Acker, vol. 2, p. 261). In this respect, the artist of this wall painting has departed from the usual preference in depicting horses.

The groom is dressed in the T'ang court costume, which is shaded with cinnabar red. Shading played an important part in the technique of wall painting; as is evident in this example, the method that reached its full development in the eighth century had already become current well before that time. (The same phenomenon is visible in the handscroll *The Thirteen Emperors*, attributed to the seventh-century painter Yen Li-pen, in the Museum of Fine Arts, Boston.)

Also to be noted in this wall painting is the earliest appearance of another device that was to be fully developed during the eighth century, i.e., the use of a wavy line to form the lower edge of the sleeves of a garment (exemplified by wall paintings in the tomb of Li Hsien [nos. 122-25]; see also Fontein and Wu, *Unearthing China's Past*, pp. 215-18).

107
Mounted guards
(west wall of corridor)

Although there exist general similarities in composition to nos. 104 and 105 on the opposite wall, this painting shows numerous subtle differences in facial expressions and postures.

104

106

107

Fig. 7

89

VIII

T'ang Tomb of Li Hsien, Prince Chang-huai

Li Hsien (A.D. 654-684) was the second son of Emperor Kao-tsung and Empress Wu Tse-t'ien. He died by his own hand and was buried at Pa-chou (in the present Pa-chung County, Szechwan Province). After the abdication of Empress Wu in 706, his remains were exhumed and brought to the imperial cemetery in the present Ch'ien-hsien County, Shensi Province, where he was reburied with all the honor due an imperial prince. According to the *New T'ang History* he was posthumously elevated in rank to crown prince Chang-huai in the spring of 711. Six months later his widow, Lady Fang, died and was buried in the same grave.

Li Hsien's tomb was excavated in 1971 and 1972. Surmounted by a tumulus measuring fifty-four feet in height, it consists of a sloping passageway, a corridor with four compartments, four airshafts, six niches, a front corridor leading into the antechamber, and an inner corridor leading into the rear burial chamber. The entire mausoleum stretches over a distance of 225 feet. In spite of the fact that the tomb was robbed at an early date, its principal feature of interest, a large number of wall paintings, remains largely intact.

The wall paintings in Li Hsien's tomb were probably first done at the time of his reburial in 706. Two archaeological reports (*Wen Wu*, 1972, no. 7, p. 48; *Wen Wu*, 1973, no. 12, p. 67) indicate that the walls were repainted five years later, although they differ in their statements as to the extent of this repainting. There seems to be no evidence that it was in any way necessitated by deterioration of the walls so soon after they were first decorated. In all probability the new paintings were made at the time when Lady Fang was interred with her husband or—even more likely—when the posthumous promotion made it necessary to adapt the subject matter to the recently conferred status of crown prince. Whether the repainting was limited to certain areas or whether it included the entire mausoleum is unclear. There is, however, a marked difference in the quality of the paintings, those in the interior being less skillfully executed than those along the walls of the sloping passageway. Whatever difference in date there may be, it is evident that all paintings were executed no later than A.D. 711.

108-112

Hunting scene

(first half of east wall of sloping passageway, covering a length of about twenty-five feet)

The principal subject matter of these five copies is a huge imperial hunting party, consisting of more than forty mounted hunters and two camels. The route along which the party proceeds is flanked by a few sparse trees and rocks that have been sketched out rather summarily. A line of five boldly drawn trees, each about five feet in height, marks the end of the long procession.

The composition of the entire scene reveals great artistic skill in rendering large groups of figures in motion. Japanese artists of the Yamato-e school excelled in depicting such groups, as is demonstrated in a masterpiece like the *Burning of the Sanjō Palace* (third quarter of thirteenth century; Museum of Fine Arts, Boston), but no convincing example of this genre survives in early Chinese handscrolls. Northern Sung copies of paintings by Chang Hsüan (early eighth century) such as *The Spring Outing of Lady Kuo-kuo* (Liao-ning Provincial Museum) or the *Ladies Preparing Newly Woven Silk* (Museum of Fine Arts, Boston) are elegant and outstanding but rather static interpretations of original T'ang masterpieces that may well have been much more dynamic and much closer in spirit to these wall paintings, all of which date from Chang Hsüan's lifetime.

It is interesting to note that many of the hunters carry "hunting leopards" or cheetahs behind them on their saddles. Figurines found in the tomb of Princess Yung-t'ai (see Watson, *Chinese Exhibition*, p. 139, fig. 275;

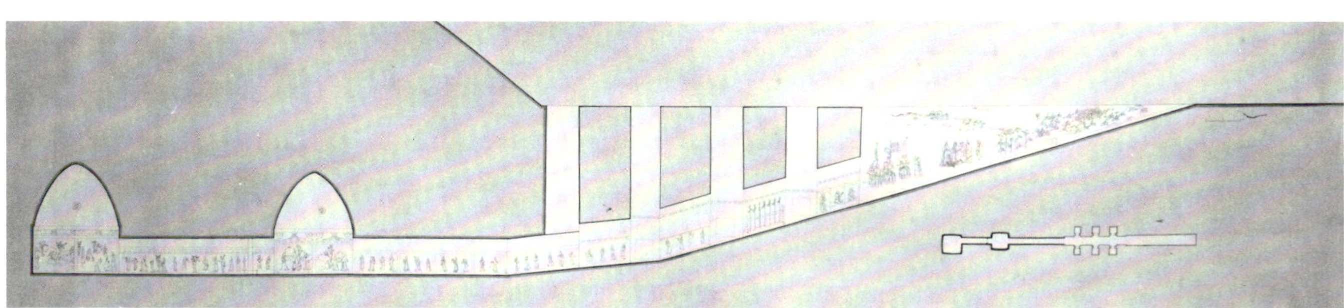

109

110

111

112

see also pp. 121-23 below) have similar cheetahs on the backs of the horses, chained to the saddle. Such trained hunting animals were imported from Samarkand and are mentioned in a list of tribute offerings presented by that country in A.D. 713 (*Schafer, Golden Peaches of Samarkand,* pp. 87-88).

Both William Watson (*Chinese Exhibition,* no. 292) and L. Carrington Goodrich ("Polo," pp. 301-302) have mistaken the whips carried by the horsemen for polo sticks. Actual T'ang polo sticks can be seen on the opposite wall, where a polo game is depicted (nos. 122-25).

The five tall trees are a remarkable work of art, drawn in a bold hand. They are matched on the west wall opposite by another group of five trees of a different species (see Shensi Provincial Museum, *Murals in the Tomb of Li Hsien,* pl. 24). Both groups are related stylistically to trees in paintings in the mid-eighth-century storehouse Shōsōin at Nara (see Shimada, *Shōsōin no kaiga,* pls. 9, 16, 18, and 23), despite the great difference in scale and a discrepancy in age of about half a century.

This manner of painting trees has a history reaching back far into China's past, both in the north and in the south. A southern tradition prevails in designs on stamped bricks portraying the "Seven Sages of the Bamboo Grove" found in a tomb of the Eastern Chin period (A.D. 317-419) at Hsi-shan-ch'iao near Nanking in 1960 (see *Wen Wu,* 1960, nos. 8/9, pp. 37-42). Examples of the northern tradition are the engraved designs on a sixth-century stone sarcophagus in the Nelson Gallery-Atkins Museum in Kansas City, Missouri (see Sickman and Soper, pls. 52 and 53), and on a stone shrine of the same period in the Museum of Fine Arts, Boston. A handscroll, *Four Scholars* (Shanghai Museum), traditionally attributed to the ninth-century painter Sun Wei, shows trees of a similar style at a later stage, although it is thought that a new manner of painting trees may have made its appearance during the latter part of the eighth century. For example, the biography of the painter Pi Hung in Chang Yen-yüan's *Li-tai ming-hua chi* states: ". . . a new departure and change from the old [style] in trees and rocks began with Hung" (Acker, vol. 2, pp. 278-79).

113 *See also color plate, p. 11.*

Officials receiving guests from afar

(east wall toward mortuary chambers)

One of the most interesting groups of figures in this tomb shows three envoys waiting to meet with three mandarins of the so-called Hung-lu Office. The mandarins are dressed in red gowns very similar to those worn by court officials shown in *The Thirteen Emperors,* attributed to Yen Li-pen (in the Museum of Fine Arts, Boston). Black gauze covers on their caps and shoes with upturned tips are also quite similar to those in that famous painting. Trailing behind each is a sash suspended from the belt, resembling that of Japanese court costumes of the Heian period, which was under T'ang cultural influence. The official on the right holds an emblem of office shaped like those associated with mandarins of the fourth or fifth rank.

At the far right stands a man with his hands folded in his sleeves. He wears fur pants and a fur hat and is possibly a delegate from the court of P'o-hai (located today in China's northeastern provinces). In Chinese historical records an envoy from the Tung-hsieh-mang tribe (in the present southwest part of China) who came to the T'ang emperor T'ai-tsung in A.D. 629 is described as wearing a black bear fur hat, a fur overcoat, and leather leggings and shoes. The emperor was sufficiently interested in this envoy's dress and appearance to order the leading painter Yen Li-te (died ca. A.D. 656) to portray him (*Old T'ang History,* ch. 147, pp. 3b-4a).

From a detailed account in an official source, the ethnic identity of the second envoy can be established with certainty as Korean. The *Old T'ang History* (ch. 149, part 1, p. 1a) gives the following description of the costumes of the North Korean kingdom of Koguryŏ: "In clothing and ornaments only the kings are entitled to the Five Colors [i.e., blue, red, yellow, black, and purple]. Their caps are made of white gauze and have a strap of white leather. Both caps and belts are decorated with gold ornaments. Mandarins of noble rank can use blue gauze for their caps, those next in rank can wear red. They attach two feathers to their caps and decorate them with gold and silver. The sleeves of their gowns and their trousers are wide and the gowns are held up by a white belt; their shoes are made of yellow leather." The distinctive headgear is also to be seen in a wall painting in the "Tomb of the Dancing Figures" at T'ung-kou (Chi-an County; formerly the kingdom of Koguryŏ near the Yalu River (see Ikeuchi and Umehara, *T'ung-kou,* pl. 10). It shows a hunter on horseback whose cap is identical with that of the second envoy here. The latter's cap is fastened to his head with a chin-strap that has been slit to accommodate his ear. A chin-strap of the same type is visible in a Northern Sung copy of a lost sixth-century handscroll depicting an envoy from the South Korean kingdom of Paekche (in the Nanking Museum; see Akiyama et al., *Arts of China,* p. 218); the headgear above the strap is too damaged to be identified. The front of the envoy's costume folds left over right, in accordance with Chinese tradition, an indication of the influence exerted by the Chinese upon Korean lifestyle. Being the only other visual record of early Korean envoys, the T'ung-kou wall painting and the Nanking Museum handscroll are of considerable interest.

The third envoy is a hawk-nosed, bald man with bushy eyebrows; he represents an ethnic type of as yet undetermined origin. An unusual aspect of this portrait is the shading applied to the envoy's costume. The same type of shading along the folds, rarely seen in Chinese figure painting, occurs on a figure on the east wall of the third compartment (see fig. 8; reproduced from Shensi Provincial Museum, *Murals in the Tomb of Li Hsien,* pl. 32). As it is also to be seen in wall paintings in Tun-huang dating from the first half of the eighth century, we may assume that it is a typical eighth-century feature (cf., for example, Gray and Vincent, *Buddhist Cave Paintings at Tun-huang,* pl. 49).

The excavation report indicates that this scene of uncommon artistic as well as documentary interest is matched by a similar group on the opposite wall, but unfortunately the latter is not illustrated in any recent publications. The great vivacity and precision with which these exotic types are portrayed—quite different from the stereotyped rendering of people of other than Han extraction by other Chinese artists—suggests that the artist of the wall painting may have been familiar with all kinds of visitors to China. Judging from Chinese literary records, there was ample opportunity to observe these people in the two capitals of the Chinese empire. However, it may bear mention that among the many responsibilities of the Hung-lu office were the following: receiving and entertaining visitors from afar and gathering information about their cultures, as well as arranging for the marriage ceremonies and funerals of members of the imperial family. Artists employed for the decoration of tombs of members of the imperial family may, therefore, have had a unique opportunity for firsthand observation of people of different ethnic origin.

113

Fig. 8

114

115

114
Honor guard
(east wall of sloping passageway)

The posture of the figure on the right, like that of a figurine guarding the tomb of the Sui general Chang Sheng (see Watson, *Chinese Exhibition,* no. 262) is apparently one associated with guard duty. He is obviously the officer in command of the soldiers, who stand on guard in three groups of three. The officer has been painted in firm, strong brushstrokes, reminiscent of the finest paintings in the tomb of Wei Chiung, the younger brother-in-law of the emperor, who died in A.D. 708 (see *Wen Wu,* 1959, no. 8, pp. 8-18). A sword like the one he holds has been preserved in the Shōsōin, where the inventory describes it as *Karatachi,* a T'ang sword (see *Treasures of the Shōsōin,* pl. 48). The soldiers all wear the same uniform consisting of a red turban and a white tunic; all are equipped with a bow and arrow case. However, instead of standing at attention or at ease, they seem to be making different gestures.

According to the excavation report, there is a similar painting on the opposite wall that has not been well preserved (*Wen Wu,* 1972, no. 7, p. 17, pl. 6a).

115
Door attendants
(east wall of fourth compartment)

Depicted in this example are two servants in a kneeling posture on a porch, carrying on a vivid conversation, while a third stands by the entrance.

The use of indoor furniture was not yet widespread in the T'ang period (Wu, "Nomadic Seat," pp. 36-43). Interiors of houses and palaces are usually bare of furniture and only a single piece is shown in wall paintings of this tomb: a garden stool on which a lady of the court is seated in Western fashion.

A scene similar to this one appears on the opposite wall (*Wen Wu,* 1972, no. 7, p. 17, pl. 7b).

116, 120, 121, and 126
Court attendants
(116: east wall, front corridor; 120: east wall, front corridor; 121: west wall, front corridor; 126: west wall, front corridor)

This pageant of court attendants covers the walls of the corridor leading into the antechamber. No. 120 is of particular interest for the two women (one of them dressed as a man) carrying trays with miniature landscapes on them. This is the earliest pictorial evidence of the art of P'en-ching (Bonsai in Japanese). A third woman holds a basket containing what appear to be silkworms.

One of the women in no. 121 carries a yellow (or gilt bronze) ewer of a typical Sassanian shape. The woman on the other side of the rock and plant holds an object resembling a large glass bowl. Nos. 116 and 126 show more variations on the same theme, except for the fact that in the latter a manservant has joined the ranks of the elegant women. His unmistakable male features prove beyond doubt that the figure in no. 120 is a transvestite.

117-119 *See color plate, p. 14.*
Court attendants
(117: east wall of antechamber, north side; 118: west wall of antechamber, south side; 119: east wall of antechamber, south side)

Inside the antechamber there are two panels with court attendants on each of the walls. On each panel are three women, a rock, and a tree, framed by cinnabar red architectural elements that give the panels the appearance of intercolumnar screen walls. No. 117 has deteriorated to such an extent that the objects carried by the court attendants can no longer be clearly discerned. In no. 119 only a Persian *p'i-p'a* can be identified. No. 118 is the most interesting and best preserved of this group. Each of the three women is differently posed. The one on the right stands stiffly, looking straight ahead. The lefthand figure, who seems to have been caught by surprise while rearranging her hair with a pin, looks up at a hoopoe bird flying past. The title given to this painting by the excavators suggests that the woman is watching the bird catching a cicada, but in the copy there is no trace of an insect to be seen. The figure in the foreground is a young woman attendant shown in a dancing pose reminiscent of a posture often struck by actors of the traditional Peking opera as they whirl their long sleeves through the air.

119

120

123

120, 121
See p. 97.

122-125 *See also color plate, p. 15.*
Polo players
(west wall of sloping passageway)

Immediately opposite the hunting scene (nos. 108-12) is a painting of horsemen playing polo in a mountainous landscape studded with trees. Landscape painting on such a large scale (covering about twenty-seven feet) is unique in the history of early Chinese art, and so is the elaborate depiction of a polo game. This is, in all probability, the earliest representation of the game after its introduction into the T'ang court during the middle of the seventh century, not from Persia, as has long been assumed, but from Tibet, convincingly demonstrated in recent research by Yin-Fa-lu (*Li-shih yen-chiu*, 1959, no. 6, pp. 41-43; no. 8, p. 20).

Riders and horses are all painted in a manner quite different from the early T'ang style exemplified by wall paintings in the tomb of Li Shou (see no. 97). Broad-shouldered costumes and wavy lines of the lower edge of the sleeves are typical features associated with the fashion and style of the early eighth century. The individualized treatment of animals seen in earlier wall paintings has now given way to a much more stereotyped, uniform manner of depiction, and the horses' bodies are sturdier.

The polo players chasing the ball that one of them is about to hit with a skillful backhand stroke are portrayed with a vivacity and intensity that convincingly conveys the excitement of the game. The players wear black boots, turban-like headgear, and costumes of different colors, indicating that they probably belong to different teams. The curved polo sticks provide the first evidence of the form of these sticks during the T'ang dynasty. By early Sung times their shape had changed into one resembling our golf clubs, as can be seen in a painting that was excavated in 1922 at Chü-lu-hsien, a city inundated and deserted in A.D. 1108, when the Yellow River changed its course. The painting was in the History Department of the old Tientsin Museum (see *Bulletin of the First Museum of Hopei Province*, vol. 5 [November 25, 1931], p. 1).

The landscape setting of the polo game suggests that the match was played in an open field rather than in a regular ball park; it must, therefore, have been a novelty. The *Feng-shih wen-chien-chi* (p. 48) relates that in the Ching-yün era (A.D. 710-711) Tibetan envoys came to the capital and gave a demonstration polo game in the grounds of the imperial theater, an indication that no special park had yet been laid out for polo. During excavations of the site of the Ta-ming Palace at Sian in 1956, a stone inscription was found marking the site of the Han-kuang Palace and a polo park constructed in A.D. 831. From this inscription it can be concluded that special parks for playing polo existed some 150 years after the game was first introduced.

Despite the excitement generated by the polo match, it is the landscape that appears to have been the artist's main interest. It comes as something of a surprise to find that at this early stage of Chinese landscape painting the landscape is more than a mere backdrop for human action. The painting differs markedly in this respect from the hunting scene on the opposite wall, where the landscape plays only a subsidiary role.

Chang Yen-yüan's *Li-tai ming-hua chi* suggests that landscape painting did not reach a mature stage of development until the time of the painter Li Ssŭ-hsün (651-716) (Acker, vol. 1, p. 156), and this mural would seem to bear out his statement. The rocks, in particular, are the creation of an artist using an advanced painting technique, as is evident from the brushwork known as "axe-cut" strokes and from the boldly defined contours. The structure of rocks and mountains shows a much greater complexity than that of the wall paintings in Li Shou's tomb (see pp. 78-89). Here the artist succeeded completely in creating an illusion of space and depth by means of a type of perspective later to be known as *p'ing-yüan* or "level distance." It is evident from his accomplishment that the art of landscape painting had evolved by this time from the primitive, symbolic phase of the Han (exemplified in the wall paintings from the tomb at P'ing-lu; see pp. 24-26 above) into the more naturalistic landscape typical of the high T'ang.

124

125

IX

T'ang Tomb of Li Chung-jun, Crown Prince I-te

LI CHUNG-JUN was born in A.D. 682, the son of Emperor Chung-tsung. His grandparents were Emperor Kao-tsung and Empress Wu Tse-t'ien. (He was originally called Chung-chao, but because it resembled the personal name of Empress Wu, his name was changed to avoid infringement upon a strict imperial taboo.) In 701 Li Chung-jun was put to death for criticizing his grandmother; four years later, when the Empress Wu fell seriously ill, Chung-tsung was able to obtain for him the posthumous title of Crown Prince I-te. It was only after the empress died later that year that his father had Chung-jun's remains exhumed and transferred to a new burying place in the imperial cemetery at Ch'ien-hsien. His tomb was officially classified as a *ling* or imperial mausoleum.

In July 1971, a team of Chinese archaeologists began the excavation of Li Chung-jun's tomb. In front of the tumulus, measuring fifty-four feet in height, stand pairs of stone columns, lions, and human figures. The mausoleum is similar in structure to the other recently excavated tombs in the Ch'ien-hsien cemetery. It consists of a sloping passageway, six compartments, seven air shafts, eight small niches, and a long corridor leading to the antechamber, connected by a rear corridor with the main burial chamber at the far end. The total length from the entrance of the passageway to the end wall of the main burial chamber is more than 300 feet.

Like the other mausoleums in the imperial cemetery, Li Chung-jun's tomb had been robbed several times in the past; in spite of these thefts more than a thousand pieces of furniture have survived intact. Although the mortuary objects are of considerable interest, the wall paintings of the tomb are more important by far.

According to the excavation report more than forty groups of figures, covering about 3,600 square feet of wall painting, have been preserved in good condition. The scale and compositional complexity of the paintings (especially those on the walls of the sloping passageway) and the quality of the brushwork are exceptional in comparison with other early eighth-century tombs. Moreover, even though paintings of architectural structures in the *chieh-hua* ("ruled and measured") manner can be found in other tombs, they never assume the monumental proportions of the towers on the wall paintings here. The landscape in the typical blue-and-green style in the background of the wall painting with the towers (no. 127) is the first actual example of this genre to be found. It is frequently alluded to in historical records of the period; likewise, the paintings of hunting animals and falcons (nos. 131, 134, and 135) are of great documentary importance.

In addition to their having unusual stylistic and iconographic features, the paintings are remarkable for their rich palette and variety of colors, a fact due probably to improvements in the technique of combining pigments. Actual samples of these colors, together with equipment for making and mixing them, were discovered in one of the compartments of the corridor. Finally, one of the most interesting discoveries in the tomb was an artist's signature on the ceiling of the antechamber. It is written in standard script in black ink and reads: "Yang Pien [-lu?]. I, Yang Pien [-lu?], wish to present this [wall painting] forever as my offering" (for a copy of the inscription, see *Kaogu,* 1973, no. 6, p. 381).

The name of the artist as written here [the reading of the third component of the name is unclear and it is not certain that it is part of the name] does not appear in any historical record. However, the *Record of Famous Painters of Successive Dynasties* mentions a painter by the name of Ch'ang Pien (Acker, vol. 2, p. 248). Since the rare character "Pien" there is identical with that of this signature, and the characters "Chang" and "Yang" are very similar in structure, it can be deduced that an error has crept into the text as a result of repeated copying in later centuries. (In fact, the next sentence contains a similar error: the character "Pien" is misprinted as "Kung.") The obvious conclusion is that the artist

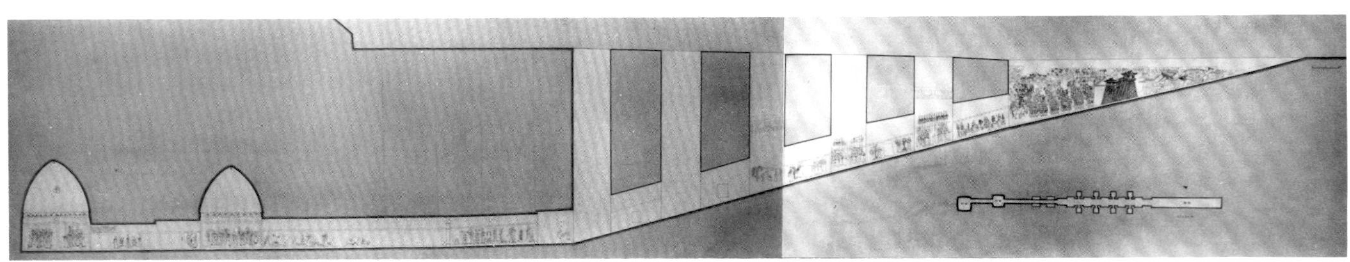

127

who placed his signature in Li Chung-jun's tomb and the person mentioned by Chang Yen-yüan are one and the same.

Chang Yen-yüan's note reads: "Ch'ang Pien excelled in [painting] landscapes, which resemble those of General Li [Ssŭ-hsün]" (Acker, vol. 2, p. 248). It is significant that the landscape painting in this tomb was done in the blue-and-green style that literary sources have always associated with Li Ssŭ-hsün. Even though the now partially damaged text of the *Stele of Li Ssŭ-hsün* by Li Yung (678-747) does not refer to the general's painting skills, the tradition of associating the blue-and-green style with this artist is so widespread that there is no reason to doubt it.

It is of interest that Yang Pien [-lu?]'s inscription is couched in language strongly reminiscent of Buddhist and Taoist dedicatory inscriptions, as we find them on stelae of the period. It suggests again that during the T'ang era there was no strict distinction between artists of temple paintings and those of tomb paintings. In Chang Yen-yüan's description of the Buddhist temple I-te-ssu, it is mentioned that this temple was originally founded during the Sui dynasty and that it was named Tz'u-men-ssu (Acker, vol. 1, pp. 291-92). The Emperor Chung-tsung renamed the temple after his late son in A.D. 705 at the time of his posthumous appointment as crown prince. On this occasion the walls of the temple were redecorated with Buddhist scenes and landscapes, the latter painted by the well-known artist Ch'en Ching-yen. All this took place during the year that preceded the construction of Li Chung-jun's tomb.

For the discussion in the following pages, Wang Jenpo's "Study of the themes depicted in wall paintings of the tomb of Crown Prince I-te" (*Kaogu*, 1973, no. 6, pp. 371 and 381-91) is gratefully acknowledged.

126

See p. 97.

127-130

Procession near the towers

(west wall of sloping passageway)

The painting represented in these copies is preceded at the entrance to the passageway by a painting of a white tiger; at its end is painted an enormous tower. The painting, about thirty feet in length, depicts a large honor guard consisting of foot soldiers, cavalry, and a train of wagons inside the city wall in front of the *chüeh* tower, a symbol of imperial status. The honor guard is, in all probability, mounted for a royal audience.

In the background of this impressive pageantry is a crisply drawn landscape in the so-called blue-and-green manner. Although the upper portion has been damaged, and the copies do not include all that has been preserved, there is enough left to make us fully appreciate the importance of this unique pictorial narrative.

No. 127 shows a compound with four *chüeh* towers, large stone structures of tapering shape surmounted by pavilion-like wooden buildings. Remains of such towers were found at the excavation site of the Ta-ming Palace at Sian, and there is evidence that similar towers existed at the Ch'ien-ling cemetery, in the immediate vicinity of this tomb. Although the history of *chüeh* towers can be traced back as far as the Western Han period, the towers in this wall painting are of typical T'ang shape. The blue roof tiles, the cinnabar red of the wooden structure, and the shape and decoration of the stone bases are almost identical with those architectural elements depicted in cave 217 at Tun-huang, which dates from the seventh century (see de Silva, *Chinese Landscape Painting*, pp. 157 and 160). The wall painting in Li Chung-jun's tomb is undoubtedly the finest architectural painting discovered in the metropolitan area.

An interesting difference between the two architectural structures in the paintings is the level from which the buildings are viewed. Those in cave 217 at Tunhuang are seen in the usual bird's-eye perspective, whereas those in Li Chung-jun's tomb are seen from below and reveal details of bracketing below the eaves. This tradition of drawing buildings in the *chieh-hua* manner with the rafters and brackets exposed continued for several centuries. It persisted even after it had become fashionable in landscape painting to adopt a more elevated viewing point showing several successive mountain ranges. The scientist Shen Kua (died A.D. 1095) criticized the famous landscape painter Li Ch'eng (died 967) for observing this anachronism in his work (*Meng-hsi pi-t'an*). The same type of "inconsistency" was noted in a late tenth-century hanging scroll discovered in an early Liao tomb (see fig. 9; reproduced from *Wen Wu*, 1975, no. 12, pl. 1).

The enormous scale of these wall paintings, and the large number of figures, horses, and chariots shown in them, has only a few parallels in the Tun-huang caves and is otherwise quite exceptional in the history of Chinese painting. Like the almost 1,000 pieces of tomb furniture, the size, quality, and subject matter of the paintings are all indicative of the imperial status of the deceased.

Fig. 9

The landscape in the blue-and-green style and the polo scene (nos. 122-25) in Li Hsien's tomb are the finest and largest examples of early T'ang landscape painting that the Chinese archaeologists have excavated. Representing two different styles of landscape painting of the same period, they offer interesting material for comparison with a number of hanging scrolls and handscrolls that carry traditional attributions to masters of the T'ang. The two most famous landscapes associated with T'ang painters are *Sailing Boats and a Riverside Mansion* and *Emperor Ming-huang's Flight to Shu,* both in the Palace Museum, Taipei. The former, probably based upon part of the handscroll *A Spring Outing* (in the Palace Museum, Peking), thought to have been painted by Chang Tzu-ch'ien of the Sui period, has a traditional attribution to Li Ssŭ-hsün; the latter has been attributed to Li Ssŭ-hsün's son Li Chao-tao. These paintings reveal either a technique too advanced for the period to which they are attributed or anachronistic features incorporated into architectural details, invalidating traditional claims of a T'ang date for them.

In *Emperor Ming-huang's Flight to Shu* the structure of the rocks is indicated in hard lines not unlike those used by the artist of the blue-and-green landscape in Li Chung-jun's tomb. The way in which colors are applied to the surface of rocks and mountains is also paralleled in the wall painting. However, the relationship between human figures and landscape is fundamentally different. In the wall painting the landscape serves merely as a backdrop, whereas in the scroll the landscape obviously dominates. The artist of the *Ming-huang* painting made an attempt to paint in an archaic fashion, but the size of the trees and the attention to detail in rendering them indicates that the painting was done at a time when landscape painting was much further developed. Of the paintings mentioned here perhaps only *A Spring Outing,* traditionally thought to have been done by a Sui master, can be attributed with confidence to the T'ang period. It may date from the later part of the eighth century.

128

130

131

131
Falconers with sparrow hawks and hounds
(north end of west wall of second compartment)

A photograph of the original painting shows that it differs in several respects from the copy. The face of the falconer (*ying-shih* or "Master of the Hawks") on the right was originally bright pink and the damaged area in the middle has been altered in the copy to show three small birds on a tree. A few leaves of the tree and the costume of the falconer on the left have been painted in a brighter green in the copy.

The birds carried by the falconers are smaller than those in no. 135 and have been identified as sparrow hawks, smaller birds of the *accipiter* family. The hound in the middle lifts its left paw to draw the attention of its master, who turns his head toward him. Both falconers point to their birds.

Falcons and other birds for hawking were often presented to the emperor by foreign envoys. They were received by th Hung-lu Office (see p. 94), which in turn handed them over to the palace officers in charge of the emperor's mews and kennels, divided into five departments, four for birds and one for hounds. According to the *Old T'ang History,* these officials were far from popular with the rural population, who resented their invasion of the countryside during the fall in trial hunts for the winter season.

Although a hunting hawk appears on a relief at Hsiao-t'ang-shan (Eastern Han period), early paintings of these birds, though often mentioned in literary sources, have not survived in large numbers. A plectrum guard of a *p'i-p'a* in the Shōsōin collection shows a hawk swooping down on a pair of geese (see Shimada, *Shōsōin no kaiga,* pls. 46-49). One of the best-known painters of hawks of the T'ang period was a member of the imperial family, Li Yüan-ch'ang, a brother of Emperor T'ai-tsung, but none of his works survives.

132
Women carrying fans

133
Two servant girls
(north end of west wall of third compartment, and south end of east wall of rear corridor, respectively)

The pairs of women in these scenes are separated by shrubs and rocks, a typical background arrangement in figure painting of the time. No. 132 shows two women carrying long-stemmed fans. In no. 133 one of the female attendants holds a Persian *p'i-p'a,* the other a ewer of Sassanian shape.

132

133

134

134
Cheetahs and their keepers
(east wall of first compartment)

This painting shows four men, each leading a cheetah on a leash. They are separated from one another by the trees and rocks that are the typical T'ang divider. Three of the keepers carry whips in the shape of golf clubs; according to the excavators this is a typical cheetah-tamer's tool. On the subject of cheetahs Edward Schafer remarks: "The scarcity of literary allusions to hunting cheetahs in the texts of that age indicates that their use must have been restricted to court circles, and for a very short time" (*Golden Peaches of Samarkand,* p. 88). This wall painting in an imperial tomb confirms his supposition.

One of the few cheetahs in Chinese painting is to be found in the thirteenth-century scroll *The Nine Songs* (Museum of Fine Arts, Boston). A light brown textile (*aya* in Japanese) in the Shōsōin collection shows a woven design of a lion and a half-naked negroid lion-tamer holding a stick similar to those in the wall painting (see *Treasures of the Shōsōin,* pp. 98-99, pl. 104). From the traces of red and green on the trees and rocks we can conclude that these were originally polychromed in bright colors, in contrast to the monochrome paintings of the cheetahs and their keepers.

According to the excavation report there is a matching scene on the opposite wall (*Wen Wu,* 1972, no. 7, p. 28).

135 *See also color plate, p. 18.*
Two falconers with goshawks
(east wall of second compartment)

Goshawks of the type shown in this monochrome painting (*accipiter gentilis*) were imported from the northeastern border regions, from the kingdom of P'o-hai and the lands of the Ho-ho. They were the most popular hunting birds in T'ang China. The two bristly, fierce-looking falconers are standing with legs slightly apart and feet spread in the posture that in China's martial arts is likened to the shape of the character "eight." The men and birds are separated by rocks and trees, the conventional divider of T'ang painting. When the artist painted the falconer on the right, he originally drew the goshawk closer to the falconer's chest, but later corrected his work, covering the first *sinopia* with whitewash. Deterioration of the surface has revealed the original drawing.

The other goshawk flaps its wings and the falconer stretches his arm to keep the bird at a distance, revealing the gauntlet covering his right hand. Such gauntlets were sometimes made of leather, as a passage in a verse of the ninth-century poet Lu Kuei-meng indicates, but his contemporary Hsüeh Feng alludes to a more elegant protection of the wrist against the bird's claws in a verse reading: "The barbarian goshawk with the green eyes treads the brocaded gauntlet." Whereas in medieval Europe falcons were usually carried on the left hand, both wall paintings and literary evidence suggest that it was more common in China to carry birds on the right.

135

136

136
Soldiers in front of a halberd rack
(east wall of second air shaft)

Twenty-four soldiers are lined up in front of a rack on which twelve halberds are placed. A painting including halberds in the first air shaft brings the total to twenty-four, the number associated with the imperial family, according to the *New T'ang History*. This painting is one of the clearest indications of the imperial rank of the deceased.

137-138
Palace attendants
(east wall of rear chamber)

Each of these copies shows nine court attendants, of whom a few are dressed as men (see above, p. 97), while the others wear elegant, long empire-style court robes of the early eighth century. The fashion of wearing the hair combed up in chignons and tufts on top of the head had been in vogue since the middle of the seventh century; it had appeared in the imperial court some twenty years earlier. Large shoes with upturned tips are another typical example of the fashion of the early eighth century; by the middle of the century they had been replaced by smaller, pointed shoes. The rather heavy eyebrows were soon to become long and thin again. A poem by the great poet Po Chü-i alludes to the later fashion in the following words: "Shoes with small tips; tightly fitting robes/The eyebrows dotted with deep purplish blue; they are thin and elongated/ People outside the palace may laugh when they see them/ But that is the fashion in makeup of the later years of the T'ien-pao-era [A.D. 742-756]" (Wu Po-lun, "Wall paintings," *Wen Wu Ching-hua*, p. 31).

The whole scene is very close in technique as well as composition to a pair of paintings in Yung-t'ai's tomb (see no. 141). Especially striking is the pose of one young woman in the center of the group on the left. She stands facing the spectator, raising her arms and holding a scarf behind her, apparently "doing her own thing," whereas all the other women are busy carrying gifts to the deceased. In the background of both groups are musicians carrying instruments.

137

138

139

139
Three servant girls
(south end of east wall of front corridor)

Of particular interest is the banana tree, a southern plant seen only in this painting.

140
Decoration of ceiling
(front corridor)

X

T'ang Tomb of Li Hsien-hui, Princess Yung-t'ai

Li Hsien-hui (A.D. 684-701) was the granddaughter of Emperor Kao-tsung and Empress Wu Tse-t'ien and the seventh daughter of Emperor Chung-tsung of the T'ang dynasty. According to the *New T'ang History* (ch. 83, p. 3652) she, like her brother Li Chung-jun was put to death by Empress Wu (see p. 104). However, this version of the events is contradicted by a mortuary inscription found in her tomb, written after Empress Wu had passed away, in which a natural cause of death is claimed. As the text was composed at the command of her father, Emperor Chung-tsung, it would seem likely, as the Chinese historian Wu Po-lun has argued, that Empress Wu should not be made responsible for the demise of this young woman (*Wen Wu,* 1963, no. 1, pp. 59-62).

In 706 Li Hsien-hui was posthumously raised in rank, being given the title of Princess Yung-t'ai. Her remains were exhumed and moved to the imperial cemetery at Ch'ien-hsien, Shensi Province, where she was reburied and reunited with her husband Wu Yen-chi in an official mausoleum located immediately adjacent to that of her grandparents.

Princess Yung-t'ai's tomb was unearthed between August 1960 and April 1962, the first of the imperial T'ang mausoleums to be scientifically excavated. The tomb consists of a sloping passageway, five compartments, six air shafts, eight niches, and a front corridor leading into the antechamber, connected by the rear corridor with the main burial chamber. Although the tomb had been robbed at an early date, more than a thousand funerary objects were found in it. Of the large number of fine figurines several were included in the exhibition from the People's Republic of China that traveled to the United States in 1974.

According to the excavation report, the base layer of the walls consisted of clay mixed with wheat chaff. It was covered by a finishing layer of white clay mixed with cotton fiber that was carefully smoothed and sized with alum. At the time of excavation most of the walls appeared in fine condition. However, due to movement of the earth, the sloping passageway had filled with soil down to the last air shaft, with the result that the wall paintings of the upper register have been almost totally destroyed. Paintings in the interior of the tomb, with only a few exceptions, have faded from exposure to humidity through the tunnels and holes dug by grave robbers.

The excavation report draws attention to the poor quality of the wall paintings in the main burial chamber of Yung-t'ai's tomb. It states that the proportions of the figures are awkward, unlike those of the paintings in

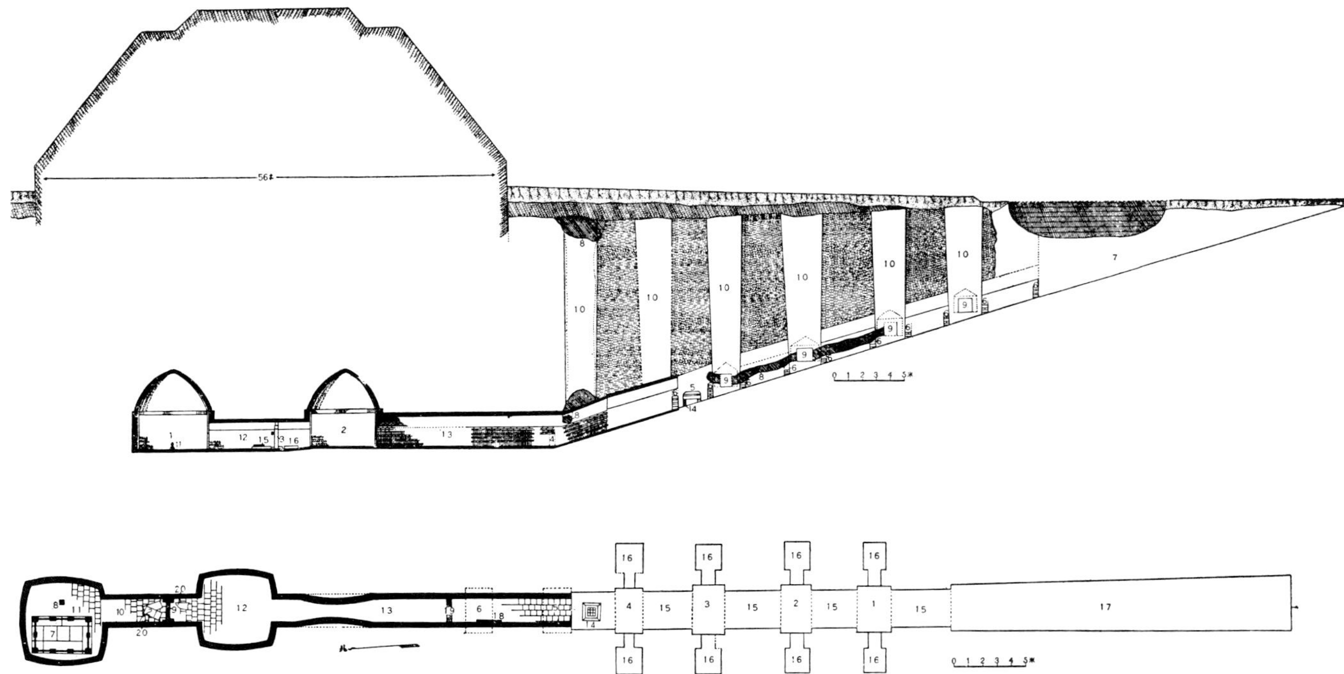

the antechamber. In spite of the fact that the walls are in good condition, most of the paintings, like those in the main burial chamber of Li Hsien's tomb, are badly faded (see Shensi Provincial Museum, *Murals in the Tomb of Li Hsien,* pls. 46-50). The cause of this deterioration has not yet been established.

141

141 *See also color plate, p. 19.*
Processions of court attendants
(east wall of antechamber)

This large wall painting is comparable in many respects to those on the end wall of the mortuary chamber in the tomb of Yung-t'ai's brother Li Chung-jun, which was built during the same year (see above, nos. 137 and 138). The painting includes two groups of nine women, of whom two are in men's costume. They all carry various objects in their hands, signifying that they may be personal attendants of the princess.

The group on the right has an exceptionally spontaneous arrangement with the women in a variety of poses, portrayed at different angles. By providing an ample margin of space around one of the figures, the artist has effectively drawn the spectator's eye to the elegant young woman in the center of the composition. The object that she carries in her hand, as yet unidentified, may possibly be a large bronze bell.

The *ju-i* scepter held vertically by a court attendant on the right is reminiscent of a figure in a wall painting in the tomb discovered at Takamatsu near Nara, Japan, in 1972. This tomb also dates from the early eighth century (*Kaogu,* 1972, no. 5, pp. 59-63). An actual *ju-i* of the period has been preserved in the Shōsōin (see *Treasures of the Shōsōin,* pls. 19 and 20).

The four women on the right, standing closely together, form a striking contrast with the spacious arrangement in the center. Such a carefully balanced composition requires great artistic vision and skill. Not surprisingly, therefore, there are numerous traces of *sinopie* indicating the extent of experimentation the artist went through before settling on the present arrangement. The composition of the group, as well as the postures of individual figures, suggests gentle, almost solemn movement, as if the women were part of a funeral procession.

The wall paintings in the tombs of Yung-t'ai and Li Chung-jun give us a vivid impression of Chinese court figure painting in the early years of the eighth century. When we compare the metropolitan style of figure painting with contemporary works of art produced in the outer provinces (at Tun-huang and in Sinkiang Province), for example, paintings reproduced in the recent publication *Cultural Relics Unearthed in Sinkiang* (see pl. 111) and the closely related painting brought back from Turfan by the Otani expedition (see Yonezawa, *Beauty in Chinese Painting,* pl. 5), we find both fashion in costume and painting style quite similar. If there is any difference at all, it is merely a matter of artistic refinement.

List of illustrations of original wall paintings

Cat. no.	*Reference:*
2	*Murals from the Han to the T'ang Dynasty*, pls. 2-3
5	*Kaogu*, 1959, no. 9, pl. 1, fig. 4
6	*Murals from the Han to the T'ang Dynasty*, pls. 10-11
	Wang-tu Han-mu Pi-hua (see Bibliography, under Hopei), pls. 11 and 21
7	*Murals from the Han to the T'ang Dynasty*, pl. 15
8	*Murals from the Han to the T'ang Dynasty*, pl. 16
9	*Wang-tu Han-mu Pi-hua*, pl. 17
10	*Murals from the Han to the T'ang Dynasty*, pls. 13-14
11	*Wang-tu Han-mu Pi-hua*, pl. 17
12	*Murals from the Han to the T'ang Dynasty*, pl. 8
15	*Murals from the Han to the T'ang Dynasty*, pl. 21
	Wen Wu, 1974, no. 1, pl. 3b
17	*Wen Wu*, 1974, no. 1, pl. 3a
26	*Wen Wu*, 1974, no. 1, pl. 2
30	*Murals from the Han to the T'ang Dynasty*, pl. 38
31	*Murals from the Han to the T'ang Dynasty*, pl. 41
	Wen Wu, 1972, no. 10, pl. 1 a-b
34	*Wen Wu*, 1974, no. 9, pl. 3
35	*Murals from the Han to the T'ang Dynasty*, pl. 43
44	*Wen Wu*, 1972, no. 12, p. 40, fig. 31
45	*Murals from the Han to the T'ang Dynasty*, pl. 47
52	*Wen Wu*, 1972, no. 12, p. 39, fig. 19
57	*Wen Wu*, 1972, no. 12, p. 40, fig. 28
60	*Murals from the Han to the T'ang Dynasty*, pl. 49
	Wen Wu, 1974, no. 9, pl. 1a
61	*Wen Wu*, 1974, no. 9, pl. 3a
62	*Wen Wu*, 1974, no. 9, pl. 1b
63	*Wen Wu*, 1974, no. 9, pl. 3c
64	*Murals from the Han to the T'ang Dynasty*, pl. 44
	Wen Wu, 1974, no. 9, pl. 1c
65	*Murals from the Han to the T'ang Dynasty*, pl. 50
66	*Wen Wu*, 1974, no. 9, pl. 4b
67	*Murals from the Han to the T'ang Dynasty*, pl. 46
68	*Wen Wu*, 1974, no. 9, p. 38, fig. 12
69	*Murals from the Han to the T'ang Dynasty*, pl. 53
71	*Murals from the Han to the T'ang Dynasty*, pl. 45

72 *Murals from the Han to the T'ang Dynasty*, pl. 55

73 *Wen Wu*, 1974, no. 9, pl. 4c

76 *Wen Wu*, 1974, no. 9, pl. 1d

78 *Wen Wu*, 1974, no. 9, p. 70, fig. 2

79 *Murals from the Han to the T'ang Dynasty*, pl. 56

80 *Murals from the Han to the T'ang Dynasty*, pl. 54

81 *Murals from the Han to the T'ang Dynasty*, pl. 58

82 *Murals from the Han to the T'ang Dynasty*, pl. 57
Wen Wu, 1974, no. 9, p. 70, fig. 3

83 *Murals from the Han to the T'ang Dynasty*, pl. 48

86 *Wen Wu*, 1974, no. 9, p. 70, fig. 5

93 *Wen Wu*, 1972, no. 12, pl. 7c

95 *Murals from the Han to the T'ang Dynasty*, pl. 52
Wen Wu, 1972, no. 12, pl. 6d

96 *Murals from the Han to the T'ang Dynasty*, pl. 51
Wen Wu, 1972, no. 12, pl. 6c

103 *Wen Wu*, 1974, no. 9, p. 81, fig. 20

104 *Wen Wu*, 1974, no. 9, p. 22

106 *Wen Wu*, 1974, no. 9, pls. 2b and 5a

108-112 *Murals in the Tomb of Li Hsien of the T'ang Dynasty*, (see Bibliography, under Shensi), pls. 1-14

113 *Murals in the Tomb of Li Hsien of the T'ang Dynasty*, pls. 25-27

114 *Murals in the Tomb of Li Hsien of the T'ang Dynasty*, pls. 28-30

116 *Murals in the Tomb of Li Hsien of the T'ang Dynasty*, pl. 33

118 *Murals in the Tomb of Li Hsien of the T'ang Dynasty*, pls. 40-42

120 *Murals in the Tomb of Li Hsien of the T'ang Dynasty*, pl. 35

121 *Murals in the Tomb of Li Hsien of the T'ang Dynasty*, pl. 37

122-125 *Murals in the Tomb of Li Hsien of the T'ang Dynasty*, pls. 16-24

127 *Murals in the Tomb of Li Chung-jun of the T'ang Dynasty*, pl. 13 (see Bibliography, under Shensi)

128 *Murals in the Tomb of Li Chung-jun of the T'ang Dynasty*, pl. 14

129 *Murals in the Tomb of Li Chung-jun of the T'ang Dynasty*, pl. 15

130 *Murals in the Tomb of Li Chung-jun of the T'ang Dynasty*, pl. 16

134 *Murals in the Tomb of Li Chung-jun of the T'ang Dynasty*, pls. 17-18

135 *Murals in the Tomb of Li Chung-jun of the T'ang Dynasty*, pl. 20

136 *Murals in the Tomb of Li Chung-jun of the T'ang Dynasty*, pls. 19, 23, and 29

141 *Murals from the Han to the T'ang Dynasty*, pls. 95-96

Measurements of the paintings

Cat. No.	(height x width in cm.)
1	33 x 278
2	23 x 193
3	88 x 45
4	120 x 259
5	90 x 178
6	89 x 254
7	50 x 81
8	49 x 129
9	39 x 243
10	92 x 256
11	96 x 65
12	91 x 65
13	131 x 86
14	194 x 193
15	68 x 133
16	110 x 92
17	132 x 260
18	132 x 262
19	98 x 102
20	125 x 204
21	88 x 116
22	98 x 131
23	131 x 262
24	132 x 133
25	130 x 132
26	137 x 201
27	191 x 300
28	165 x 172
29	132 x 64
30	200 x 82
31	95 x 726
32	70 x 269
33	17 x 36
34	17 x 36
35	17 x 36
36	17 x 36
37	17 x 36
38	17 x 36
39	17 x 36
40	17 x 36
41	17 x 36
42	17 x 36
43	17 x 36
44	17 x 36
45	17 x 36
46	17 x 36
47	17 x 36
48	17 x 36
49	17 x 36
50	17 x 36
51	17 x 36
52	17 x 36
53	17 x 36
54	17 x 36
55	17 x 36
56	17 x 36
57	17 x 36
58	17 x 36
59	17 x 36
60	17 x 36
61	17 x 36
62	17 x 36
63	17 x 36
64	17 x 36
65	17 x 36
66	17 x 36
67	17 x 29
68	17 x 36
69	17 x 36
70	17 x 36
71	17 x 25
72	17 x 36
73	17 x 36
74	17 x 36
75	17 x 36
76	17 x 36
77	17 x 36
78	17 x 36
79	17 x 36
80	17 x 36
81	17 x 36
82	17 x 36
83	17 x 36
84	17 x 36
85	17 x 36
86	17 x 36
87	17 x 36
88	17 x 36
89	17 x 36
90	17 x 36
91	17 x 36
92	17 x 36
93	46 x 132
94	17 x 80
95	66 x 101
96	66 x 102
97	231 x 229
98	131 x 160
99	65 x 76
100	56 x 65
101	80 x 83
102	64 x 66
103	125 x 89
104	198 x 200
105	195 x 199
106	196 x 132
107	207 x 319
108	98 x 132
109	107 x 129
110	154 x 190
111	194 x 162
112	191 x 225
113	187 x 245
114	224 x 337
115	167 x 237
116	152 x 138
117	263 x 218
118	267 x 196
119	265 x 186
120	119 x 217
121	127 x 198
122	197 x 161
123	198 x 129
124	167 x 237
125	229 x 161
126	182 x 155
127	283 x 275
128	313 x 268
129	260 x 218
130	351 x 226
131	178 x 151
132	179 x 132
133	130 x 144
134	192 x 398
135	164 x 147
136	293 x 300
137	195 x 197
138	191 x 194
139	139 x 230
140	226 x 166
141	186 x 419

Bibliography

Academia Sinica, Institute of Archaeology. *Hsin Chung-kuo ti k'ao-ku shou-huo* [Archaeological discoveries in New China]. Peking: Wen Wu Press, 1962.

Academia Sinica, Institute of Archaeology. *T'ang Ch'ang-an Ta-ming-kung* [The Ta-ming Palace of the T'ang at Ch'ang-an]. Peking: Science Press, 1959.

Academia Sinica, Institute of Botany. *Chung-kuo kao-teng chih-wu t'u-chien* [Illustrated encyclopedia of Chinese botany]. Peking: Science Press, 1972, vol. 2, p. 84, fig. 1897.

Acker, William R. B. *Some T'ang and Pre-T'ang Texts on Chinese Painting*. Leiden: E. J. Brill (vol. 1, 1954; vol. 2, 1975).

Akiyama Terukazu et al. *Arts of China*. Tokyo: Kōdansha, 1968, vol. 1.

An Chih-min. "Notes on the wall paintings of the Han tomb at Wang-tu" (text in Chinese). *Kaogu*, 1957, no. 2, pp. 104-107.

An Chin-huai and Wang Yu-kang. "On the Han dynasty stone relief tomb and the wall painting tomb unearthed at Ta-hu-t'ing in Mi-hsien" (text in Chinese). *Wen Wu*, 1972, no. 10, pp. 49-55.

Barnhart, Richard. "Survivals, Revivals, and the Classical Tradition of Chinese Figure Painting." *Proceedings of the International Symposium on Chinese Painting*. Taipei: National Palace Museum, 1972, pp. 143-250.

Bulling, A. "Historical Plays in the Art of the Han Period." *Archives of Asian Art* 21 (1967-68), pp. 20-38.

Bunker, Emma, C. "Early Chinese Representations of Vimalakīrti." *Artibus Asiae* 30 (1968), pp. 28-52.

Cahill, James. *Chinese Painting*. Ascona: Skira, 1960.

Chang An-chih. "On the painting *Spring Outing of Lady Kuo-kuo*" (text in Chinese). *Wen Wu*, 1961, no. 12, pp. 67-68.

Chang Yen-yüan. *Li-tai ming-hua chi* [Record of Famous Painters of Successive Dynasties]. (Chin-tai-pi-shu edition; reprinted in 1630s by Mao Chin of the Chi-ku-ko Studio; for Acker translation, see above).

Ch'ang Jen-hsia. *Han-hua i-shu yen-chiu* [Studies in Han wall paintings]. Shanghai: Shanghai Press, 1955.

Chavannes, Edouard. *Mission archéologique dans la Chine Septentrionale*, vol. 1: *La sculpture à l'époque des Han*. Paris: Ernest Leroux, 1913.

Chaves, Jonathan. "A Han Painted Tomb at Loyang." *Artibus Asiae* 30 (1968), pp. 5-27.

Ch'en P'an. "A note on the plant *chieh-huo*, also known as *chin-tien*" (text in Chinese). *Ta-lu tsa-chih* 52, no. 6 (June 1976), p. 256.

Ch'en Yin-k'o. *Sui T'ang chih-tu yüan-yüan lüeh lun kao* [Origins of political systems of the Sui and T'ang dynasties]. Hong Kong: Chung-hua (1974 reprint).

Cheng Hsüan (annotator). *Chou Li* [Ritual of Chou]. Shanghai: Commercial Press (1929 reprint).

Cheng Hsüan and K'ung Ying-ta (commentators). *Li Chi* [Book of Rites]. Shanghai: K'ai-ming (1935 reprint).

Cheng Shao-tsung. "On four Han ink-stones" (text in Chinese). *Wen Wu*, 1964, no. 10, pp. 42-43.

Cheng Te-k'un. "The Exhibition of Archaeological Finds in China." *Journal of the Institute of Chinese Studies of the Chinese University of Hong Kong*, no. 2 (1974), pp. 401-23.

Chia-yü-kuan City, Archaeological Team. "Ancient cliff drawings by the nomads of Kansu" (text in Chinese). *Wen Wu*, 1972, no. 12, pp. 42-43, pl. 9.

Chia-yü-kuan City, Archaeological Team. "Han tombs with brick paintings at Chia-yü-kuan" (text in Chinese). *Wen Wu*, 1972, no. 12, pp. 24-41.

Chin Wei-no. "On the date of the Eastern Han tomb with wall paintings at Holingol" (text in Chinese). *Wen Wu*, 1974, no. 1, pp. 47-50.

Chou Li. See Cheng Hsüan.

Chu Chang-ch'ao et al. *T'ang Yung-t'ai kung-chu mu pi-hua chi* [Wall paintings from the tomb of Princess Yung-t'ai of the T'ang dynasty]. Peking: People's Fine Art Press, 1963.

Fan Yeh et al. *Hou Han Shu* [History of the Later Han Dynasty] (Po-na edition).

Fang Chuang-yu. "The development of the plow since the Warring States Period" (text in Chinese). *Kaogu*, 1964, no. 7, pp. 355-63.

Feng Yen. *Feng-shih wen-chien-chi* [Record of things heard and seen by Mr. Feng]. Shanghai: Chung-hua (1958 reprint annotated by Chao Chen-hsin).

Fischer, Otto. *Die chinesische Malerei der Han-Dynastie*. Berlin: Neff, 1931.

Fontein, Jan, and Pal, Pratapaditya. *Oriental Art*. Boston, Museum of Fine Arts, 1969.

Fontein, Jan, and Wu Tung. *Unearthing China's Past*. Boston: Museum of Fine Arts, 1973.

Fushimi, Chūkei (annotator). *Unki Shōgun Ri Shikun no hi* [The stele of the Yün-mao general Li Ssŭ-hsün]. Tokyo: Nigensha, 1959.

Goodrich, L. Carrington. "Polo." *T'oung Pao*, vol. 61, nos. 4/5, pp. 301-302.

Gray, Basil, and Vincent, J. B. *Buddhist Cave Paintings at Tun-huang*. London: Faber and Faber, 1959.

Hirth, Friedrich. *The Native Sources of the History of Chinese Pictorial Art* (pamphlet). New York, 1917.

Historical Memoirs. See Ssŭ-ma Ch'ien.

History of the Later Han Dynasty. See Fan Yeh et al.

Ho Chih-kang. "On the date and the identification of the occupant of the Eastern Han tomb at Wang-tu" (text in Chinese). *Kaogu*, 1959, no. 4, pp. 197-200.

Honan Province, Archaeological Team, Bureau of Culture. "Excavation of a Western Han tomb with wall paintings at Lo-yang" (text in Chinese, English abstract). *Kaogu Xuebao*, 1964, no. 2, pp. 107-25.

Honan Province, Department of Culture. "Two large Han tombs with wall paintings and with stone reliefs discovered at Ta-hu-t'ing in Mi-hsien, Honan Province" (text in Chinese). *Wen Wu*, 1960, no. 4, pp. 49-50 and 51-52.

Hopei Province, Commission for the Preservation of Ancient Monuments, and the Peking Museum of History. *Wang-tu Han-mu Pi-hua* [Wall paintings of the Han tomb (no. 1) at Wang-tu]. Peking: Ancient Chinese Art Press, 1955.

Hopei Province, Department of Culture. *Wang-tu Erh-hao Han-mu* [Wall paintings of the Han tomb no. 2 at Wang-tu]. Peking: Wen Wu Press, 1959.

Hsia Nai. "Constellations painted on the ceiling of a Western Han tomb at Lo-yang" (text in Chinese). *Kaogu*, 1965, no. 2, pp. 80-90; no. 9, p. 479.

________. "Notes on archaeological work in Tun-huang" (text in Chinese). *Kaogu*, 1955, no. 1, pp. 3-4.

Hsiang Ta. "The Ch'ang-an of the T'ang Dynasty and the Civilization of the Western Regions." *Yenching Journal of Chinese Studies*, monograph series no. 2 (1933), pp. 74-81.

Hsin Chung-kuo K'ao-ku shou-huo. See Academia Sinica.

Hsü Chien. *Ch'u-hsüeh chi* (encyclopedia). Peking: Chung-hua (1962 reprint).

Hsü Heng-pin. "Note on an early fourth-century ceramic model of plowing and harrowing unearthed at Lien-hsien, Kuang-tung province" (text in Chinese). *Wen Wu*, 1976, no. 3, pp. 75-76.

Huang Sheng-chang. "The wall paintings of the Eastern Han tomb at Holingol, Inner Mongolia, and questions of history and geography" (text in Chinese). *Wen Wu*, 1974, no. 1, pp. 38-46.

I-nan. See Nanking Museum.

Ikeuchi Hiroshi and Umehara Sueji. *T'ung-kou*. Tokyo: Zauho Press, 1940.

Inner Mongolian Archaeological Team and the Museum of the Inner Mongolian Autonomous Region. "An important Eastern Han tomb with wall paintings found at Holingol, Inner Mongolia" (text in Chinese). *Wen Wu*, 1974, no. 1, pp. 8-23.

Institute of Chinese Medicine (Research Division). "Exercising postures on silk fragments discovered in Han tomb no. 3 at Ma-wang-tui" (text in Chinese). *Wen Wu*, 1975, no. 6, pp. 6-13, 63.

Kansu Provincial Museum. "Archaeological report of three Han dynasty tombs found at Mo-chü-tzu, Wu-wei county, Kansu Province" (text in Chinese). *Wen Wu*, 1972, no. 12, pp. 9-23.

Kansu Provincial Museum. "The practice of the legalist's policy in the Ho-hsi area as reflected in the brick paintings of the tombs of the Wei to Chin periods discovered at Chia-yü-kuan" (text in Chinese). *Wen Wu*, 1976, no. 2, pp. 83-86 and pl. 1.

Kansu Provincial Museum. "The subject matter and artistic value of the tomb wall paintings of the Wei and Chin dynasties at Chia-yü-kuan" (text in Chinese). *Wen Wu*, 1974, no. 9, pp. 66-69.

Kao, George. *Chinese Wit and Humor*. New York: Sterling Publishing Co., 1974.

Kaogu Xuebao. Peking: Science Press (1953-).

Kishibe Shigeo. "The origin of the p'i-p'a" (text in Japanese), pp. 117-56; "On European opinions of the Western origin of the p'i-p'a" (text in Japanese), pp. 157-68. *Tōyō Ongaku senshū*. Tokyo: Society for Research in Asiatic Music, 1968.

Kita-Kyūshū City Museum. *Chūka Jimmin Kōwakoku Kantō Hekigaten* [Wall paintings from the Han and T'ang periods from the People's Republic of China] (fully illustrated). Kita-Kyūshū: City Museum, 1974.

Kohara, Hironobu. "On Admonitions of the Instructress" (text in Japanese). *Kokka*, no. 908, pp. 17-31; no. 909, pp. 13-27.

Kuo Mo-jo. "An investigation of the wall paintings in a Western Han tomb at Lo-yang" (text in Chinese). *Wen-wu Ching-hua*, no. 3 (1964). [Peking: Hsin-hua shu-tien], pp. 27-29.

Lawton, Thomas. *Chinese Figure Painting*. Washington, D.C.: Smithsonian Institution, 1973.

Li Ch'iu-shih. "On the structure of the two tombs of Crown Prince Chang-huai and I-te" (text in Chinese). *Wen Wu*, 1972, no. 7, pp. 45-50 and 58.

Li Fang et al. *T'ai-p'ing yü-lan* (encyclopedia). Shanghai: Chung-hua, 1960 (reprinted from the Han-fang-lou edition, vol. 4).

Li I-yu et al. *Nei-meng-ku ch'u-t'u wen-wu hsüan-chi* [Cultural relics unearthed in Inner Mongolia]. Peking: Wen Wu Press, 1963.

Li Tao-yüan. *Shui-ching-chu* [Commentary on the Water Classic]. Peking: Classical Literature Press, 1955 (reprinted from *Yung-lo ta-tien*).

Li Wen-hsin. "Three ancient tombs with wall paintings discovered in Liao-yang" (text in Chinese). *Wen Wu*, 1955, no. 5, pp. 15-51.

Liao-ning Provincial Museum. *Liao-ning-sheng po-wu-kuan ts'ang hua chi* [Illustrated catalogue of paintings in the Liaoning Provincial Museum]. Peking: Wen Wu Press, 1962.

Lin Shu-chung. "On the date of the wall paintings of the Han tomb at Wang-tu" (text in Chinese). *Kaogu*, no. 4, 1958, pp. 66-71.

Liu Hsü. *Chiu T'ang shu* (Po-na edition).

Liu Ling-ts'ang. *T'ang-tai jen-wu hua* [Studies in T'ang figure painting]. Peking: Classical Art Press, 1958.

Lo Che-wen. "Some ancient buildings depicted in the wall paintings of the Han tomb at Holingol" (text in Chinese). *Wen Wu*, 1974, no. 1, pp. 31-37.

Lo Tsung-cheng. "Report on the excavation of a tomb of the Chin dynasty in I-hsing, Kiangsu Province" (text in Chinese). *Kaogu Xuebao*, 1957, no. 4, pp. 83-106.

Lu Kuei-meng. *Lei-ssŭ-ching* (Chin-tai-pi-shu edition, reprinted in the 1630s by Mao Chin of the Chi-ku-ko Studio).

Ma Ts'ai. *Ku K'ai-chih yen-chiu* [Studies on Ku K'ai-chih]. Shanghai: People's Fine Art Press, 1958.

Maeda, Robert J. "Chieh-hua: Ruled-line painting in China." *Ars Orientalis* 10 (1975), pp. 123-41.

Matsumoto Eiichi. *Tonkō-ga no Kenkyū* [Research on Tunhuang murals]. Tokyo: Tōhō Bunka Gakuin, 1937.

Min Wen-ju. "Preliminary report on archaeological works in the Ho-hsi area, Kansu Province" (text in Chinese). *Kuo-hsüeh Quarterly* (Peking University) 7, no. 1, pp. 115-40.

Murals from the Han to the T'ang Dynasty. Peking: Foreign Language Press, 1974.

Nagahiro Toshio. "On the mural engravings of *Seven Sages of the Bamboo Grove* and Yung Ch'i-chi, dating between the Chin and the Sung dynasties" (text in Japanese). *Kokka*, no. 857 (August 1963), pp. 15-21.

Nanking Museum and Commission for the Preservation of Ancient Monuments of Nanking City. "Archaeological report on the Southern dynasty tomb discovered at Hsi-shang-ch'iao, Nanking, and the stamped brick decoration of the tomb" (text in Chinese). *Wen Wu*, 1960, nos. 8-9, pp. 37-42.

Nanking Museum and Cultural Bureau of Shantung Province. *I-nan ku hua-hsiang-shih mu fa-chüeh pao-kao* [Excavation report on an ancient tomb with engraved stone decoration discovered at I-nan]. Shanghai: Hsin-hua Press, 1956.

National Palace Museum. *Three Hundred Masterpieces of Chinese Paintings in the Palace Museum Collection*. Taichung: Ku-kung po-wu-yüan, 1959, vol. 1.

Needham, Joseph. *Science and Civilization in China*. Cambridge: University Press, 1970, vol. 3.

New T'ang History. See Ou-yang Hsiu.

Old T'ang History. See Liu Hsü.

Ou-yang Hsiu et al. *Hsin T'ang Shu* [New T'ang History]. Peking: Chung-hua, 1975 (reprint from Po-na edition).

Palace Museum. *Ku-kung po-wu-yüan ts'ang-hua* [Paintings in the Palace Museum Collection]. Peking: People's Fine Art Press, 1964, vol. 2.

Po Chü-i. *Po shih ch'ang-ch'ing chi* [Collected works of Po Chü-i]. Ed. Ma Yüan-tiao (author's preface in 809 A.D.). Peking: Classical Literature Press, 1955, vol. 1, pp. 38-39.

Rowland, Benjamin. "A note on Wu Tao-tzu." *Art Quarterly* 17, no. 2, (summer 1954), pp. 144-50.

Schafer, Edward H. *The Golden Peaches of Samarkand*, Berkeley and Los Angeles: University of California Press, 1963.

Shanghai Museum. *Shang-hai po-wu-kuan ts'ang li-tai shu-fa hsüan-chi* [Calligraphy in the Shanghai Museum collection]. Peking: Wen Wu Press, 1964, vol. 1.

Shansi Province, Commission for the Preservation of Ancient Monuments. "A Han dynasty tomb with wall paintings at Tsao-yüan village in P'ing-lu County, Shansi Province" (text in Chinese). *Kaogu*, 1959, no. 9, pp. 462-63.

Shen Kua. *Meng-hsi pi-t'an* [Miscellaneous notes of Meng-hsi]. Peking: Chung-hua, 1957 (reprint annotated by Hu Tao-ching).

Shensi Province, Commission for the Preservation of Archaeological Monuments. "Excavation of the tomb of Princess Yung-t'ai of the T'ang Dynasty" (text in Chinese). *Wen Wu*, 1964, no. 1, pp. 7-33.

Shensi Province, Commission for the Preservation of Ch'ien Ling, Ch'ien-hsien. Comments on the article "Notes on the structure of the tombs of Crown Princes Chang-huai and I-te" (text in Chinese). *Wen Wu*, 1973, no. 12, pp. 67-68.

Shensi Provincial Museum and Commission for the Preservation of Archaeological Monuments. "Excavation of the T'ang tomb of Li Shou at San-yüan, Shensi Province" (text in Chinese). *Wen Wu*, 1974, no. 9, pp. 61, 71-88.

Shensi Provincial Museum and Commission for the Preservation of Archaeological Monuments. "Studies on the wall paintings of the tomb of Li Shou of the T'ang Dynasty" (text in Chinese). *Wen Wu*, 1974, no. 9, pp. 39, 89-94.

Shensi Provincial Museum and Commission for the Preservation of Archaeological Monuments of Shensi Province. *Murals in the Tomb of Li Chung-jun of the T'ang Dynasty*. Peking: Wen Wu Press, 1974.

Shensi Provincial Museum and Commission for the Preservation of Archaeological Monuments of Shensi Province. *Murals in the Tomb of Li Hsien of the T'ang Dynasty.* Peking: Wen Wu Press, 1974.

Shensi Provincial Museum and T'ang Tombs Archaeological Team, Bureau of Culture and Education of Ch'ien-hsien. "Excavation of the T'ang tomb of Crown Prince Chang-huai" (text in Chinese). *Wen Wu,* 1972, no. 7, pp. 13-25.

Shensi Provincial Museum and T'ang Tombs Archaeological Team, Bureau of Culture and Education of Ch'ien-hsien. "Excavation of the T'ang tomb of Crown Prince I-te" (text in Chinese). *Wen Wu,* 1972, no. 7, pp. 26-31.

Shih Hsio-yen. "I-nan and Related Tombs." *Artibus Asiae* 22, no. 4 (1959), pp. 277-313.

Shimada Shūjirō et al. *Shōsōin no Kaiga* [Paintings in the Shōsōin]. Tokyo: Nihon Keizai Shimbun, 1968.

Shōdo Meikan [Connoisseurship in calligraphy]. Osaka: Nihon Tosho Shuppansha, 1954.

Shōdo Zenshū [Illustrated history of calligraphy]. Tokyo: Heibonsha, 1967, vol. 26.

Shōsōin. *Treasures of the Shōsōin.* Tokyo: Asahi Shimbun, 1965.

Sian City, Commission for the Preservation of Ancient Monuments. "Western Han bronzes unearthed at Kao-yao ts'un, San-ch'iao-chen, Sian" (text in Chinese). *Kaogu,* 1963, no. 2, pp. 62-70.

Sickman, Laurence, and Soper, Alexander. *The Art and Architecture of China.* Baltimore: Penguin Books, 1960.

Silva, Anil de. *The Art of Chinese Landscape Painting.* New York: Crown Publishers, 1967.

Sinkiang Museum. *Cultural Relics Unearthed in Sinkiang.* Peking: Wen Wu Press, 1975.

Sirén, Osvald. "Central Asian Influence on Chinese Painting of the T'ang Dynasty." *Ars Asiatiques* 3, no. 1 (1956), pp. 3-21.

________. *Chinese Painting: Leading Masters and Principles.* London: Lund Humphries, 1956, vol. 3.

________. *History of Early Chinese Painting.* London: de Medici Society, 1933, vol. 1.

Soper, Alexander. "Life Motion and the Sense of Space in Early Chinese Representational Art." *Art Bulletin* 30, no. 3 (September 1948), pp. 167-86.

________. "A New Chinese Tomb Discovery: The Earliest Representation of a Famous Literary Theme." *Artibus Asiae* 24, no. 2 (1961), pp. 79-86.

Ssŭ-ma Ch'ien. *Shih Chi* [Historical Memoirs] (Po-na edition).

Study Group for the Han Silk Manuscripts from Ma-wang-tui. "Report on the military map found in Han tomb no. 3 at Ma-wang-tui" (text in Chinese). *Wen Wu,* 1976, no. 1, pp. 18-32.

Tanaka Ichimatsu and Yonezawa Yoshiho. *Hakubyō-ga kara suiboku e no tenkai* [Development from outline sketches to ink paintings]. Tokyo: Kōdansha, 1975.

Tokyo and Kyoto National Museums. *Archaeological Treasures Excavated in the People's Republic of China* (exhibition catalogue). Tokyo and Kyoto: National Museums, 1973, pl. 110.

Tomita Kojirō. "A Chinese Sacrificial Stone House of the Sixth Century A.D." Museum of Fine Arts, Boston, *Bulletin* 40 (December 1942), no. 242, pp. 98-110.

________. "Portraits of the Emperors, a Chinese Scroll Painting Attributed to Yen Li-pen." Museum of Fine Arts, Boston, *Bulletin* 30, no. 177 (February 1932), pp. 1-8.

Tun-huang Research Institute. "Chin tombs discovered at Tun-huang" (text in Chinese). *Kaogu,* 1974, no. 3, pp. 191-99.

Tun-huang Research Institute. *Tun-huang pi-hua* [Wall paintings of Tun-huang]. Peking: Wen Wu Press, 1959.

Wang Jen-po. "Study of the themes depicted in wall paintings of the tomb of Crown Prince I-te of the T'ang dynasty" (text in Chinese). *Kaogu,* 1973, no. 6, pp. 371, 381-93.

Wang Po-min. *Wu Tao-tzu.* Shanghai: People's Fine Art Press, 1958.

Wang Yeh-ch'iu. "On the need for research materials on the history of ink-stones" (text in Chinese). *Wen Wu,* 1964, no. 1, pp. 49-52.

Watson, William. *The Chinese Exhibition.* Toronto: Royal Ontario Museum, 1974.

Wen Wu (formerly *Wen-wu ts'an-k'ao tzŭ-liao*). Peking: Wen Wu Press (1950-).

Wen Yu. *Ssŭ-ch'uan Han-tai hua-hsiang hsüan-chi* [Han decoration from the Ssŭ-ch'uan Province]. Shanghai: Chu-lien Press, 1955.

Wu Ch'i-chün. *Chih-wu ming-shih t'u-k'ao* [Studies in Chinese botany]. Shanghai: Commercial Press (1933 reprint), pp. 254-55.

Wu Jung-tseng. "Life in Eastern Han society as reflected in wall paintings of the Han tomb at Holingol, Inner Mongolia" (text in Chinese). *Wen Wu,* 1974, no. 1, pp. 24-30.

Wu Lung-tseng. "Inspection of the ruins of the Han castle at Ta-pu-t'u village, east of Hu-ho-hao-t'eh of Inner Mongolia" (text in Chinese). *Kaogu,* 1961, no. 4, pp. 212-13; no. 6, p. 340.

Wu Po-lun. "The tombstone of Princess Yung-t'ai of the T'ang dynasty" (text in Chinese). *Wen Wu*, 1963, no. 1, pp. 59-62.

________. "Wall paintings and pottery figurines unearthed from the tomb of Princess Yung-t'ai of the T'ang dynasty" (text in Chinese). *Wen Wu Ching-hua*, no. 3 (1964) [Peking: Hsin-hua shu-tien].

Wu Tung. "From Imported 'Nomadic Seat' to Chinese Folding Armchair." Museum of Fine Arts, Boston, *Bulletin* 71 (1973), no. 363, pp. 36-51.

Yao Chien. "The tomb chamber structure and wall paintings of the Han tomb at Wang-tu, Hopei Province" (text in Chinese). *Wen Wu*, 1954, no. 12, pp. 47-63.

Yao Tsui. *Hsü Hua P'in* [Continued classification of painters]. Shanghai: Po-ku-chai, 1922 (reprinted in the 1630s by Mao Chin of the Chi-ku-ko Studio; for Acker translation, see above).

Yin Fa-lu. "The importation of Polo from Tibet into the capital Ch'ang-an in the T'ang dynasty" (text in Chinese). *Li-shih yen-chiu*, 1959, no. 6, pp. 41-43; no. 8, p. 20.

Yonezawa Yoshiho. *Beauty in Chinese Painting*. Tokyo: Heibonsha, 1958.

Yü Chien-hua. *Chung-kuo hui-hua-shih* [History of Chinese painting]. Shanghai: Commercial Press, 1937, vol. 1.

Yü Chien-hua et al. *Ku K'ai-chih yen-chiu tzŭ-liao* [Research material on Ku K'ai-chih]. Peking: People's Fine Art Press, 1962.